Putting Interpretation on the Map

AN INTERPRETIVE APPROACH TO GEOGRAPHY

Heidi Bailey

For Kyle and Matthew

May you see many places and journey through many spaces.

Acknowledgments

First and foremost, I wish to express my gratitude to my friend and mentor, Karissa DeCarlo, lead interpreter at Timpanogos Cave National Monument in Utah. Her thoughts, ideas, and opinions are infused into every page of this book. She made valuable suggestions and served as my inside source for many of the National Park Service materials that I used in my research. Due to Karissa's extensive travels and her eye for exhibits, I was able to include a variety of photos from many different places. This book would not have happened without her encouragement as a friend and her expertise as an interpreter.

I also wish to extend my thanks to the many other people who contributed to researching and writing this book:

My family—Rocco, Taryn, Judy, Eric, and Ellen—for their love, patience, support, and spending time with the little one.

Superintendent Keith Payne and the staff and volunteers at Florissant Fossil Beds National Monument, especially Jeff Wolin and Sally McCracken-Maertens.

My professors at West Virginia University, especially Dave Smaldone, Greg Elmes, and Robert Burns.

National Park Service Harpers Ferry Center, especially Tom Patterson, for their beautiful maps and rich map-making resources.

Gary Bremen at Biscayne National Park for sharing his materials on living maps.

Dr. Joseph Kerski for reviewing this book with a geographer's eye. His comments and suggestions were essential to the completion of this book.

Geoff Irons at REI for his wonderful course on using a map, compass, and GPS.

Jennifer Armstrong, Jason Bird, George Brown, Nicole Poisson, and the National Park Service for contributing map images.

Catherine McCarthy for her expertise on designing podcasts and cell phone tours.

Members and supporters of the Global Geoparks Network, especially Wesley Hill of the GSA.

My editor, Paul Caputo, for his guidance and patience over the last few years.

And finally, Junior Ranger Chandler for her inspiration.

Contents

interpPress

Copyright © 2009
National Association for Interpretation
ISBN-13: 978-1-879931-26-8

**NATIONAL ASSOCIATION FOR
INTERPRETATION**

The National Association for Interpretation
is a private nonprofit [501(c)3] organization
and professional association. NAI's mission
is: "Inspiring leadership and excellence to
advance natural and cultural interpretation
as a profession." For information, visit www.
interpnet.com.

Cover photo illustration by Ove Tøpfer.

Foreword

The early 21st century is an age of contrasts. More people are getting out in the field than ever before, and opportunities for doing so have never been more numerous. Back when I was growing up in western Colorado, for example, not one person went mountain biking or jet-skiing, and yet those activities are enjoyed by thousands each month. However, an intimate connection to landscape and place is less likely to be a part of our common human experience than ever before. We laughed in the movie "Vacation" when Chevy Chase drove for days to reach the edge of the Grand Canyon, took a breath, and said, "Okay, kids, back in the car!" Yet how often do we fail to allow ourselves to really experience a place? As someone who has been involved with technology for my entire career, I am all for using digital photography, GPS, and other tools in the field. Yet how often do I and others take a photograph and then plot our course in the GPS for the next waypoint? Do we even have the skills to experience place any longer? And if we cannot, so what? Why is it important to do so?

Putting Interpretation on the Map makes it clear that the reason to reconnect with place and landscape is not simply to enhance the experience of a visitor to a park, museum, historical battlefield, or wilderness area. To make certain that we even have natural places to interpret means they need to be protected. Only those who have had experiences with these and other special places— especially as children—will ensure that legislation is put there to protect them. And interpreters help provide those experiences. Heidi Bailey brings a wealth of ideas and skills to interpreters that some argue we possessed when we all worked the land and were intimately acquainted with the climate, vegetation, animals, soil, water, and other characteristics of a place. She brings these skills to the forefront through the discipline of geography.

Putting Interpretation on the Map should dispel popular opinion that equates geography with memorizing long lists of imports, exports, capes, bays, and state capitals. As this book makes abundantly clear, geography is key to understanding and grappling with all of the key issues of our time—energy, water, natural hazards, migration, urbanization, habitat, climate, and more, at scales from local to global. Holistic thinking has always been a part of interpretation as it has always been a part of geography. As environmental scientist David Orr said, "We need people to think big picture, to pick apart the trivial from the important."

For decades, interpreters have been geographers in action, applying the geographic themes of place, movement, region, human-environment interaction, and location to real places, real events, and real people. This book identifies the numerous points of intersection between geography and interpretation. It offers the interpreter a wealth of resources, projects, and ideas for how to expand these points into a multifaceted surface that can enrich any park, museum, or other program. At the same time, I would argue that this book also offers the geography educator ways to more purposefully incorporate interpretation and fieldwork into instructional practice both in schools and in after-school programs.

This book also makes it clear that geography is action-oriented, framed by the ethics of sustainability, which drives interpreters to affect society one individual at a time. In an age when many of the general public are discouraged from taking action, this book offers hope that individual interpreters can and do make a difference. From the story of Sally at Florissant Fossil Beds National Monument to the everyday work-world of thousands of interpreters, this book shows that interpretation is needed now more than ever. In the wake of widespread, documented declines in student fieldwork and public connection to the landscape in this electronic age, interpretation is shown to not only enhance experiences at museums, parks, and other sites, but also as the key to reconnecting the public to landscape and to history. It is my belief that this book will help interpreters and the people they serve to develop a deeper appreciation for these special places they steward, and enable the public to take action to protect them through their actions and through legislation. The optimism that Ms. Bailey has about humans as a "resource of knowledge and creativity" shines throughout the book. In fact, she offers solid advice for constructing educational spaces that encourage people to get involved in Earth-related issues rather than throwing up their hands because the issues that confront us are simply too complex to solve.

Why should an interpreter or a visitor care about such issues? Because it is precisely, as is made clear in the book, in parks and museums where many people first start to realize the fragile state of Earth affairs, and start appreciating history, place, and landscape in the geographic sense of the words.

It is essential to connect people to the landscape, to conservation, and to outdoor education. We have paid paltry attention to these things in our formal educational system, and we do so at our peril. Landscape and place make a deep impression on us, especially acute during the impressionable time of childhood. As a child, I got to know the Grand Valley, from its orchards to the canals that watered them, from the barren Mancos Shale hills to the one-meter-wide cracks we called "lemon squeezers" where we crawled through the sandstone at the base of the Colorado National Monument. As well documented by Louv and others, if the human-land connection is not made at an early age, then it is no wonder we lose acres of land per minute to urban sprawl, why lakes are unfit to swim in, and—choose the environmental issue you are most passionate about and fill in the blank here.

Interpreters can help galvanize citizen science as never before, helping people to gather data in what is sometimes referred to as "volunteered geographic information." The connection between interpretation and geography is not just a nice thing, or a useful thing—it is a *critical* thing, critical not only for that local site where the public and the interpreter intersect, but for the region and for the planet.

Putting Interpretation on the Map lives up to its title to provide guidance about how to more effectively use maps in analog and digital form. If you like maps, you will love this book. If you don't like maps, (as a geographer I admit, sadly, that there are such people), then this book might help you develop at least a recognition that they may be a useful foundation for your work. Nowadays, people are using some computer-based technologies when they are out in the field, whether it is a cell phone that takes photographs or a portable music player that can download podcasts. Ms. Bailey encourages the incorporation of these and other technologies into geotechnologies such as GPS, Geographic Information Systems, and Remote Sensing. In these days when anyone can create a web-based map, she anchors the generation of map-based products in cartography and geodesy to ensure quality.

Wonderfully illustrated, the book's tone and the personal stories make for enjoyable and informative reading. I am confident that this book will play a positive role in making a difference in conservation and education. Yet it all begins with you, the reader. What action will you take to incorporate these principles into your teaching, your interpretation, and in your own life?

—Joseph J. Kerski

"Once in a place, that journey to the far interior of the psyche begins or it doesn't. Something must make it yours…"
—Frances Mayes, *Under the Tuscan Sun*

A 12-year-old girl walked into the visitor center at Florissant Fossil Beds National Monument in Colorado. She wore a hip-length vest studded with dozens of National Park Service Junior Ranger badges. Park patches spilled across the back of her vest, and even more attached themselves to a sash about her shoulders.

The girl stepped up to the front desk and presented the park ranger with a letter. In the typed note, she addressed the rangers and volunteers of Florissant Fossil Beds National Monument:

Six years ago a volunteer at the front desk gave me my first Junior Ranger program. My family and I visited this national monument on our second trip "out west." I happened upon my first program this trip. We were traveling in an R.V. then, as we do now. I was only six years old at the time when I completed

Connecting Minds and Hearts to Places

Above: *Snow Canyon State Park, Utah*

my first Junior Ranger program.

The Junior Ranger programs I have done have informed me about the environment and history of our country, and the culture of the people who have lived here before us. Some visitors to the national parks just get their stamp at the visitor center and leave—that is not why our national parks are here! They are here to educate and provide enjoyment to the public. The Junior Ranger programs help me, my parents, and everyone who does these programs to get involved with the national park they are visiting, including park rangers, the history, and the environment.

I have been driven to get more badges after my first at Florissant Fossil Beds National Monument, one became 10, 10 became 25, and so on. Six years and over 200 Junior Ranger badges later, I am still on my journey to visit every single national park and do their Junior Ranger program to learn more about them.

Thank you for getting me started.

Junior Ranger ~ Chandler

Chandler's story began with a visit to a place. She "happened upon" a program that caused a place to captivate her mind and inspire her heart. This is the fundamental goal of interpretation, a profession devoted to connecting minds and hearts to places.

Interpreters are tour guides, museum docents, exhibit designers, and park rangers. They work for zoos, heritage centers, tourist bureaus, and public agencies. Some are staff. Some are volunteers. All are faced with the challenge of creating opportunities for visitors and guests to make a connection with a place.

Interpreters have a difficult time finding references that are designed to meet their needs. Unlike teachers, interpreters do not have whole class periods or entire semesters to communicate an idea. Thus, educational books on subjects like geography are often not suited to meet their needs.

Interpreters need short activities and easy to describe concepts that can be incorporated into a 15-minute program or an exhibit that is read in 30 seconds. This book is designed to meet that need. The intended audience includes front-line interpreters, exhibit designers, site planners, and land managers who are seeking new opportunities for connecting minds and hearts to places.

My hope for this book is that you will find a new idea that inspires a story like the one about the girl who happened upon a place.

2

HEIDI BAILEY

Interpreters are Geographers

"At least as important as good resource management is environmental education. And in dealing with issues so fundamentally rooted in space, the language of geography is what's spoken."

—ESRI brochure

The geographer Yi-Fu Tuan once said, "If we think of space as that which allows movement, then place is pause."

Take a moment to think of a place where you like to pause—a place where you enjoy stopping to look, to listen, or to inhale a breath of fresh air. What is this place? Where is it located? Why is it special to you? How would you describe what this place means to you?

Now think about the last time you went on a trip. Where did you go? Try to visualize the entire journey. How much ground did you cover? What landscapes did you see? What spaces did you travel through? Did you meander across a broad area or stick to a narrow path?

Visitors to interpretive sites come to see places and experience

Above: *Horseshoe Bend, Glen Canyon National Recreation Area, Arizona*

spaces. By learning what places and spaces are and how to communicate their meaning, we can become better interpreters. As you read this book, I encourage you to keep in mind the words of Yi-Fu Tuan: "If we think of space as that which allows movement, then place is pause."

Let's begin our journey by pausing to take a more in-depth look at the meaning of place and space.

Place and Space

A place is a location bound to a meaning. A single place may mean many things to many people. Every one of us develops emotional and intellectual connections to places—our home, a childhood haunt, a nearby park, or a faraway land. This type of attachment is known as *sense of place*. Interpretation fosters these attachments by creating opportunities for people to form connections to places.

Space is defined as having extent, area, or volume and can exist at a variety of scales. The area between molecules in a drop of water is a type of space, as is the area within the rooms of your home. Space exists within the boundaries of a national park, between the Earth and sky, and across the solar system. In this book, we will consider a special type of space known as a *landscape*.

A landscape is a meaningful portion of land. Every person, place, or object interacts spatially with the surrounding landscape. Homes are *next to* one another, rivers flow *between* mountains, a park is *north* of the city. The interaction of things across a landscape can create a meaning very different from the meanings of the individual elements. For instance, a watershed is created by the complex interactions that occur between a river, a forest, and a snow-capped peak.

A goal of interpretation is to connect visitors to the meaning and spirit of places. Yet interpretive sites are more than collections of natural formations, historic buildings, or ancient ruins. These places interrelate spatially within a landscape that possesses a meaning of its very own. People relate to large spaces in a fundamentally different way than they relate to individual places. Thus, every place should be put in context of the larger space in which it resides.

The study of the relationship between place and space is part of a science known as geography.

The Geography of Places and Spaces

Geography is the science that allows us to unearth the intriguing relationships that occur between the places and spaces that surround our lives. As interpreters, we routinely tell the historical story of our sites, yet we often overlook the

A place is a location bound to a meaning. A single place may mean many things to many people. Monument Valley Navajo Tribal Park.

HEIDI BAILEY

geographical story. This may be because we think of geography as a dull subject that involves the rote memorization of state capitals or the political borders of countries. But geography doesn't begin and end with maps that show where places are located. Geography is so much more.

Geography is about visualizing large spaces, getting acquainted with special places, and connecting to the earth as a whole. Geography represents the visible and invisible lines that define our communities and public lands. Geography separates cultures or encourages them to mingle. Geography is defined by how humans perceive the natural world and the choices we make to develop or preserve places. Geography can be a mental landscape that we hold in our individual or collective memories—a favorite childhood retreat or a place of worship.

Every day we dwell, work, play, and rest in individual places. Sometimes we embark on journeys through large spaces, enlarging the boundaries of our world, expanding the geographies of our minds. Our personal geographies change every day when we take a walk down a new street, read about a long-ago place, or see images of a far away space.

We may think of geography as just the lay of the land, but geography is also people—the relative location of you and me, the gulf of space between you and your visitors. Interpretation is a tool that allows us to build bridges connecting special places to the personal geographies of visitors.

Our Inner Geographies

Geography is different for every person. Because we have a place that we live, we have a certain point of view from which to see other places. Individuals categorize a place based on their idea of what it should look like. For instance, a person from the eastern United States may have one idea of what a mountain looks like, while a person from the western United States may have a very different idea of what a mountain looks like. A visitor that is accustomed to the steep, rocky mountains of the West may look at the small, gentle mountains of the East and categorize them as hills.

Every one of us possesses mental constructs called *schema representations* that help us decide what an object or place is. Schema representations are abstractions of the features common to many different but similar environments. They provide a blueprint or framework that allows us to identify an unfamiliar setting. This allows us to imagine a space we have not seen by applying this mental blueprint when visualizing a new environment. For example, the schema for a national forest may conjure an image of trees, trails, campsites, and ranger stations.

Geography is also about people. A cultural demonstration in La Gamba, Costa Rica, is pictured here.

The many types of landscapes in a single region may sometimes confuse visitors. National parks, wilderness areas, state forests, and private recreation areas may be located near one another, making it difficult to recognize different types of land.

Visitors may not realize that the missions of different agencies can drastically affect the layout of a landscape. For instance, the multiple-use zones within a national forest can result in a different type of landscape than in a national park. This can lead to confusion and disappointment when a visitor's mental image of one type of protected area is influenced by another.

Interpretation has the power to provide visitors with an appreciation of the differences between places and spaces, allowing them to refine their inner geographies and close the gap between the real and imagined world.

Closing the Geography Gap

Our inner geographies often bear little resemblance to the actual world. Americans, in particular, are notoriously bad at geography. The National Geographic Society reports that of the nine countries that participated in the 2002 Global Geographic Literacy Survey, Americans from the ages of 18–24 ranked next to last.

The survey quizzed over 3,000 young adults in Canada, France, Germany, Great Britain, Italy, Japan, Mexico, Sweden, and the U. S. Out of 56 questions, Americans averaged 23 correct answers. Only 30 percent could find the Pacific Ocean on a map. In 2006, another National Geographic poll found that half of Americans in this same age group were unable to locate New York on a map.

We know we're bad at geography—we even make fun of ourselves in popular media. On the *Tonight Show*, Jay Leno used to do a segment called "Jaywalking." He

Images of Asian Highlands

When you hear the words "Asian Highlands," do you imagine Genghis Khan and his nomadic warriors riding across the vast steppes? Wisps of wind-blown snow swirling above Mt. Everest?

Mosaics and Monocultures

When you picture a healthy forest, do you imagine lots of big trees? Actually, a healthy forest ecosystem is a mosaic, which means that it is made up of lots of mini habitats: big trees and small trees, old plants and young plants. It's just like a healthy society—you need all sorts of people!

When you think of a desert, what do you picture? The Chihuahuan Desert is much more than sand and cactus. The Chihuahuan Desert is the largest desert in North America and includes a variety of habitats that are home to an impressive diversity of aquatic and mammal species.

Visitors categorize a place base on their idea of what it should look like. Above: *Cheyenne Mountain Zoo, Colorado.* Two images at right: *Mesilla Valley Bosque State Park, New Mexico.*

would hit the streets and ask people questions like, "What state is the city of New York in?" Leno knew that questions on geography were certain to generate humorous responses. Of course, his victims were not entirely to blame. If Jay Leno walked up to me on the street, my mind would probably go blank, too.

And geography is a challenging subject. Pick up any atlas lying around your home or office, and it was probably out-of-date before it was even printed. Conflicts and shifts in power throughout the world cause borders to move and names to change. The Soviet Union collapsed, the Berlin Wall fell, African countries have tossed aside colonial names and restored traditional ones.

But the geography of the U.S. has not changed much in my lifetime, and yet as a former resident of New Mexico, I can say from personal experience that many Americans do not know that this state is part of our country. In fact, New Mexico magazine has an entire column devoted to this phenomenon. Every month, people share humorous stories about how "One of our 50 is missing."

So the question is, why are we so bad at geography?

The author of *Don't Know Much About Geography*, Kenneth Davis, offers some possible reasons. He says that geography is often taught in a way that squeezes all of the fun out of it. Imagine a history class that just focuses on memorizing dates or a science class that forces you to remember the scientific names of plants and animals. As any good interpreter or educator knows, focusing on dry facts and scattered bits of information will quickly quell most anyone's interest in a subject.

Yet geography is often taught in exactly this way—memorizing the locations of countries, the names of state capitals, or studying the per capita income of a region. *Boring.* There is always a story behind all of this information—fascinating reasons why people and places are the way they are today.

When Geography Changed History

The president of the American Geographical Society says, "Geography is to space what history is to time." While knowing *when* a story happened provides a historical context and makes it easier to visualize events, knowing *where* a story happened provides a geographical context and makes it easier to visualize the place where the events occurred.

We often think of history as just the story of people: presidents and generals, explorers and soldiers, settlers and families. Yet history is defined by other major players, and geography is chief among them. The lay of the land is an important factor in the outcome of many historical events. The relative location, size, and shape of landforms influence both our

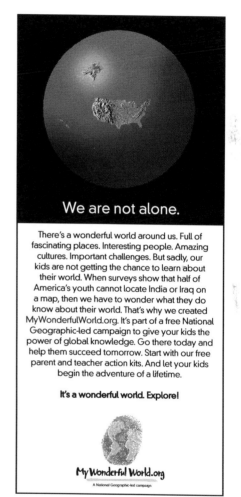

To learn more about closing the geography gap, visit National Geographic at www. mywonderfulworld.org.

history and our present. Weather patterns, geological formations, and biological diversity determine the location of settlements, battlefields, and political borders.

Incorporating the geographical element into interpretive stories reveals the many ways our lives are intertwined with places. For instance, the outcome of the most costly battle of the Civil War—the battle of Gettysburg—was determined in large part by the local terrain.

During the battle, Union forces positioned themselves on a ridge known as Cemetery Hill. Although this low-lying ridge may seem insignificant to people visiting Gettysburg today, the landform played an important role in the outcome of the battle. During an event known as Pickett's Charge, Confederate forces marched across a grassy field and became easy targets for the Union troops stationed on higher ground. Only about 100 of the 12,000 men who started the charge made it to Cemetery Hill. The rest retreated or fell.

Interpreters at Gettysburg National Park tell this and other stories through programs that focus on the geographic factors that contributed to the outcome of the battle and ultimately, the war. The Electric Map program at the park is presented in a gym-size room with a three-dimensional model of the battleground on the floor surrounded by bleachers. The program uses multi-colored electric lights embedded in the model to show the movement of troops with respect to natural landforms.

The Cyclorama program at Gettysburg immerses visitors in a 360-degree depiction of the landscape and emphasizes the relationship between battle events and topography. According to one visitor study, people who attend these programs report increased understanding of the events that took place at Gettysburg.

Programs like the ones at Gettysburg National Park relate historical events that occurred long ago to elements of the landscape that visitors can still see today. Incorporating geography into interpretation is a powerful way to create new opportunities for people to connect with places.

Interpreters are Geographers

One of the great things about geography is that it applies to every subject. Geography literally means *to describe the Earth*. If you interpret a subject that exists on, in, or above the Earth, you are a geographer. Your story can be about people, plants, animals, rocks, fossils, or anything else that you find on, in, or above the Earth. Your challenge is to be a good geographer. This book will help you do just that. Let's start by shaking things up a little.

NPS / JOHN HEISER

Geography influenced the outcome of the Civil War. *Cemetery Ridge at Gettysburg National Military Park, Pennsylvania.*

ROCCO BLASI

Geography applies to every subject. *Glacier National Park, Montana.*

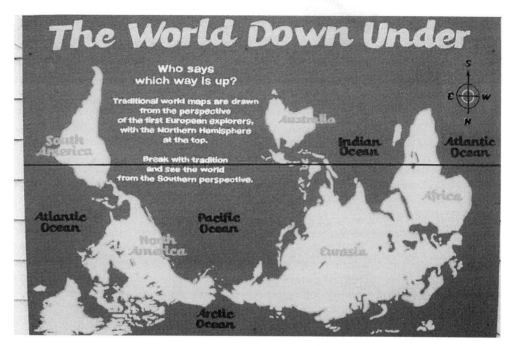

The World Down Under

Who says which way is up?

Traditional world maps are drawn from the perspective of the first European explorers, with the Northern Hemisphere at the top.

Break with tradition and see the world from the Southern perspective.

South America

Atlantic Ocean

Pacific Ocean

North America

Arctic Ocean

Australia

Indian Ocean

Atlantic Ocean

Africa

Eurasia

Geography can be used to challenge visitors' perceptions. Left: *Wichita Zoo, Kansas.* Below: *Ecological Footprint Map.*

A good geographer realizes that things aren't always what they appear to be. We are all raised with maps and globes that place north at the top. Yet the Earth is a sphere—it doesn't really have a top or bottom. If you have a ball lying around, pick it up and look at it. If the ball has lines or labels, it may appear to have a top or bottom, but does it really?

The Earth rotates on an axis, which gives us a convenient way to choose a top and bottom. But we are hurtling through outer space—couldn't the South Pole just as easily be the top? Take a look at the maps on this page—does this look like the Earth that you know and love?

View more perception-busting maps at http://www.worldmapper.org/.

Now that you have discovered that you are actually a geographer, I encourage you to shake things up by challenging people's perceptions and putting the fun back into geography. You can do this by telling people the fascinating story of your place, encouraging people to think geographically, emphasizing the personality of places, and finding connections to people's lives.

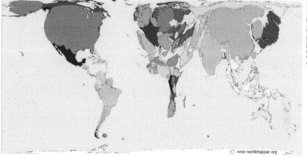

Wondering how to get started?

Almost every place has a name. Often, this name is a clue to a place's personality. Places may be named for the shapes of landforms, native words, famous historical figures, local nicknames, myths, obscure stories, or even as a metaphor for something else. You can start your journey as a geographer by researching the name of a special place. Talk to local people, check the library, and look at records in a public land office. Use this information as the starting point for a geo-interpretive program.

Names are often a clue to a place's personality. *Mesilla Valley Bosque State Park, New Mexico.*

A River by Any Other Name
Un Río por Cualquier Otro Nombre

Over the years the Rio Grande has been known by many names. Southern Tiwa Indians called it "Pehla Uhle," (peth-la uth-lah) meaning Big River. The first Spanish settlers in 1540 named it "Río de Nuestra Señora" (River of Our Lady). Twenty-eight years later, three British sailors dubbed it "River of May." Mescalero Apache called it "Tu' ichinii," or "Red Water."

Modern Mexicans call the river "Rio Bravo," from the Spanish for "wild." Other names reflect the same untamed nature: Río Turbio (Turbulent River) and Río Caudaloso ("carrying much water").

The first person to use the name Rio Grande was probably Juan de Oñate, a Spanish explorer who reached its banks near El Paso, Texas in 1598.

KARISSA DECARLO

Resource managers ask the public to understand abstract spatial concepts such as habitat corridors. *Canada Parks.*

A Geo-Interpretive Program

Interpretive programs that focus on geography can help visitors develop a sense of place and form a connection to the landscape as a whole. Resource managers are increasingly asking the public to understand more abstract spatial concepts such as habitat corridors, historical landscapes, cultural regions, and watersheds. Yet, lacking understanding of how people learn about place and space, many sites do not currently facilitate geographic learning. This creates a need for geographic interpretation.

This chapter closes with an example of geo-interpretive program (see the sidebar on the opposite page). As you read this script, imagine that you are viewing a three-dimensional model or a virtual map that displays the landscape described in the program. You will discover how the complex interactions between different places can provide water to a large city.

The Where of Water

Let's explore how the geography of this area made the city of Albuquerque, New Mexico, what it is today. In this program, you will discover that *what* happens is directly related to *where* it happens.

In 1706, settlers founded Albuquerque on the banks of the Rio Grande River at present day Old Town. The town flourished and grew into the largest city in New Mexico because of one important resource—ground water. The geography of the area influenced the development of Albuquerque by creating this valuable resource.

You have probably noticed that Albuquerque—the largest city in the state—thrives in the middle of a desert. This area has been home to many cultures throughout history—the Pueblo, Spanish, American, and many others. These people all shared a need to find a reliable source of water in the midst of this dry climate.

Three geographic features—often appreciated only for their scenic beauty—have contributed to the availability of water and thus the development of Albuquerque. These features are: the Sandia Mountains, the Rio Grande river valley, and the West Mesa.

Let's look over the city to the east at the Sandia and Manzano mountains. Does anyone know what the words *sandia* and *manzano* mean? Watermelon and apple. I encourage you to view a sunset while you are here and think about how the mountains earned their names.

The Sandia Mountains formed when a large block of granite pushed up out of the Earth and tipped on its side. It's just like when you step on a loose brick and one side of the brick pops up. You can see that Albuquerque faces the bold, tipped-up side. The other side of the Sandias is smoother and much less dramatic. Think of this mountain range as the lip of a giant tub or sink.

Now we will go to the west side of Albuquerque to see the West Mesa. Does anyone know what *mesa* means? Table. You can see that this is a large flat area of land that has been lifted up like a table. Close by are five volcanoes that also indicate that the Earth's crust has been pushing up in this area. This forms another lip of our imaginary sink or tub.

What do you think happened in the middle? As the surrounding areas pulled apart and lifted up, the middle sank down. But Albuquerque is not at the bottom of a great trench, and that is because of the work of the Rio Grande River, which flows between the Sandia Mountains and the West Mesa.

We usually think of rivers carving out great valleys, but the Rio Grande has done just the opposite. It has valiantly worked to fill in a cave-in of the Earth's crust. The sediment deposited by the Rio Grande is filled with tiny holes. These holes absorb water. Imagine placing a large sponge in the bottom of the sink or tub rimmed by the Sandias and the West Mesa. This sponge forms the aquifer that provides Albuquerque with 100 percent of its water.

Next time you turn on a faucet, I encourage you to think about how the geography of this area has enabled you to do that. The arrangement of the Sandia Mountains, the West Mesa, and the Rio Grande River has provided you with this valuable resource.

The people of Albuquerque thrive due in large part to the water supply made possible by the geography of the area. Thus, *what* happened is directly related to *where* it happened.

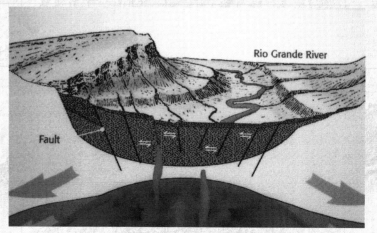

The spatial arrangement of the Sandia Mountains (left), the Rio Grande River (center), and the West Mesa (right) provides water to the city of Albuquerque, New Mexico. *Mesilla Valley Bosque State Park, New Mexico.*

3

Themes of Place

Above:
Natural Earth III

"Despite their diversity, every one of the major issues confronting our planet has one thing in common—they all have a spatial or geographic component. Interpreters have a deep sense of place and are most at home when discussing the historical, environmental, geologic, or other spatial aspect of a particular piece of geography…. Indeed, the entire discipline of interpretation is closely aligned with the tenets of geography education, grappling with themes of movement, regions, location, and place."
—Joseph Kerski (*Legacy* May/June 2007)

Interpreters define a theme as the main point, principal message, or big idea they want to convey to an audience.

I like to think of a theme as a miniature story—the answer to a mystery, the refrain to a song, the revelation of a secret, the punch line to a joke. A theme is much more than a topic. A theme is a one-line story that reveals the actions, personality, value, or significance of a subject and why we should care about it.

Themes guide visitors in their perception of a place or

landscape. Themes guide interpreters in their depiction of a place or landscape. In this chapter, we will look at how geographic themes apply to the interpretation of places and spaces. In addition, we will consider how interpretive trends are changing the way we portray places and spaces.

The Five Themes of Geography

A set of guidelines for geography education was created in 1984 by the National Council for Geographic Education and the Association of American Geographers. Five subject headings were developed as part of these guidelines. These relate to the topics of movement, region, human/environment interaction, location, and place. A convenient mnemonic for remembering these five subjects is MR HELP. In this section, we will consider how these topics can be developed into the following interpretive themes:

> Patterns of Geography Move the World
> Regions Unite a Diversity of Places
> Humans and the Environment
Influence Each Other
> Locations Show the Positions of Places
> Every Place has a Unique Personality

An explanation of these themes and activity ideas for each follow:

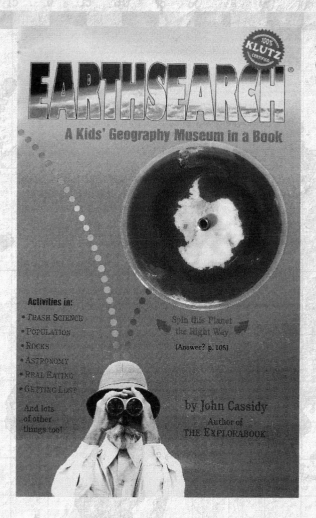

Find ideas for your geography exhibit in Earthsearch.

Earth Search

Are you thinking about designing a geography exhibit? Track down a copy of *EarthSearch: A Kid's Geography Museum in a Book* (1994), published by Klutz, a subsidiary of Scholastic, Inc. Here is the description from the back of the book:

> This is a 98-page hands-on geography museum designed for residents of the third planet from the sun. It's meant to be done, not just read, since it's full of activities and exhibits. Its subject? Geography—that means everything from the tip of your nose going out.

This book will have you drawing contour lines on Whoopi Goldberg's face and stretching Arnold Schwarzenegger's head out like a map projection in no time. (We will learn about contour lines and map projections in Chapter 4.)

Trade goods, languages, beliefs, science, art, music, and stories moved along the Silk Road between Italy and China. *Harvard University Museums, Massachusetts.*

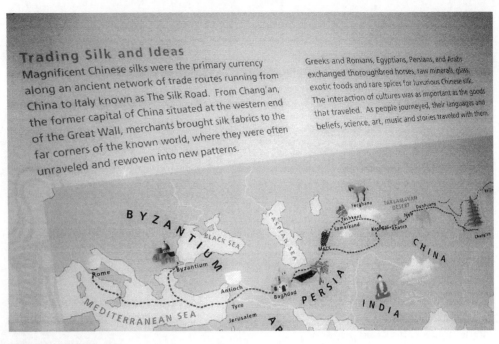

Trading Silk and Ideas
Magnificent Chinese silks were the primary currency along an ancient network of trade routes running from China to Italy known as The Silk Road. From Chang'an, the former capital of China situated at the western end of the Great Wall, merchants brought silk fabrics to the far corners of the known world, where they were often unraveled and rewoven into new patterns.

Greeks and Romans, Egyptians, Persians, and Arabs exchanged thoroughbred horses, raw minerals, glass, exotic foods and rare spices for luxurious Chinese silk. The interaction of cultures was as important as the goods that traveled. As people journeyed, their languages and beliefs, science, art, music and stories traveled with them.

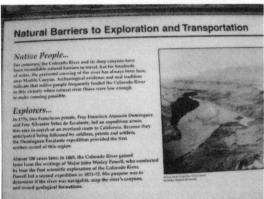

The Colorado River created a natural barrier to movement in the southwestern U.S. *Vermillion Cliffs National Monument, Arizona.*

Patterns of Geography Move the World.

Patterns exist that enable animals, matter, people, products, and ideas to move from one place to another. The way things move in and out of a place is an important factor in determining what a place is like.

At one time, physical geography was the most important factor in determining the way things moved over the surface of the Earth. Land bridges, ocean currents, and wind patterns determined the spread of people, animals, and plants. Physical barriers often prevented the sharing of skills and ideas between cultures.

Today, patterns of movement are largely defined by the geography of technology. Roads, airports, and access to computers determine how products and ideas move from place to place. Dams affect the flow of rivers while cities and roads alter the way animals and plants move through an ecosystem.

Interpreting these patterns of movement is an important avenue for showing visitors how their everyday lives are influenced by places both near and far.

Activity Ideas:

1) Compare human transportation systems to natural movement systems such as erosion and tides.

2) Discuss how geographic obstacles and language barriers affect the movement of people and ideas.

3) Ask participants to plan out a route for delivering a message to another place, or for an animal to migrate to a different area.

Regions Unite a Diversity of Places.
Geography is often thought to be defined by political boundaries. Yet many of the traits that places share are not contained within these artificial borders. Regions are areas that share certain unifying characteristics that stretch across political boundaries. By focusing on this theme, interpreters can foster a pride of region in local residents and promote an understanding of region in visitors.

Regions can provide a starting point for learning about other places. The characteristics that define a region give us a frame of reference for comparing and contrasting other parts of the world. Sometimes far away places share characteristics that allow us to form connections to places we have never seen.

Interpreters can use the similarities and differences between regions to help people identify with communities at both the local and global level.

Activity Ideas:

1) Show participants a map of an area and see how many different regions they can name: cultural, recreational, climatic, ecological, etc.

2) Identify a region and have people list things that make it distinctive. Be sure to look for subtle similarities rather than just stereotypical ones.

3) Immerse visitors in a region using interactive cultural displays, ethnic foods, etc.

Different regions can share similar characteristics. The Colorado Rocky Mountains and the Central Asian Himalayas share similarities in setting, climate, and latitude. *Cheyenne Mountain Zoo, Colorado.*

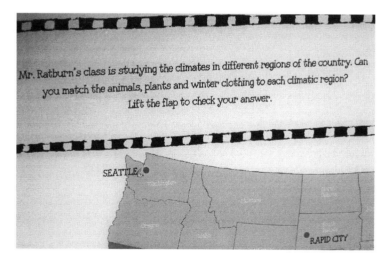

Regional differences influence the animals, plants, and weather found in different parts of the U.S. *Boston Children's Museum, Massachusetts.*

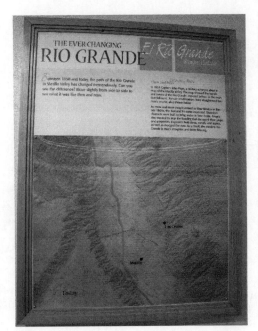 

In the early 1800s, the Rio Grande River influenced the locations of human settlements. In turn, human modifications along the river have straightened the Rio Grande's course over time. In this exhibit, visitors can see the changes in the landscape by moving from side to side. *Mesilla Valley Bosque State Park, New Mexico.*

Humans and the Environment Influence Each Other.

Human use and misuse of the environment is a common theme in interpretation. When people interact with their surroundings, they create both positive and negative effects. But the other part of this story is that the environment influences humans. Our surroundings have a profound effect on our lifestyles and daily choices.

For instance, climate determines the food we eat, the clothes we wear, and the kind of houses we build. Climate also influences the decisions we make on how to develop the land. In arid regions, humans construct dams and irrigate fields to create a more hospitable place to live. This can, in turn, alter the environment in ways that affect the local or global climate.

Understanding this cycle of human-environment interaction is an important step in reducing our negative impacts on the Earth and making these interactions more sustainable.

Activity Ideas:

1) Show visitors old and new photos of a place and ask them to verbalize how people have changed the landscape.

2) Have participants identify how people have adapted to the surroundings in order to survive.

3) Ask visitors how the conditions at your site affected their travel plans and their decisions on what to bring with them.

Locations Show the Positions of Places.

The position of places and people on the earth can be pinpointed on a map. This is known as absolute location and is often the focus of visitor orientation programs. Relative location, on the other hand, refers to how places relate to one another and how they are interconnected.

Every interpretive story happens somewhere. As interpreters, we can show how the absolute or relative location of a place influenced the outcome of that story. Perhaps the events unfolded at a particular spot in a desert landscape or near a prominent landscape feature such as a mountain range.

This theme is about knowing that what happens is related to where it happens. Try to imagine your interpretive story occurring at another location. How would the outcome be different?

Activity Ideas:

1) Familiarize visitors with your site by asking them to locate features on a map such as the highest mountain, headwaters of a river, or nearest town.

2) Teach basic map and compass skills and have participants practice by determining the locations of landmarks.

3) Encourage visitors to identify the many ways that your site is connected to places both near and far.

What is Geodesy?

Geodesy is the science of measuring the size and shape of the Earth and precisely locating points, or coordinates, on the earth. These geodetic coordinates can tell us exactly where we were, where we are, and where we'll be when we get there. NOAA uses the Global Positioning System (GPS) to maintain the National Spatial Reference System, which provides all the reliable, global positioning data used to make nautical charts.

AMAZING GEODESY!

The science of precisely measuring and locating points on the Earth is known as geodesy. This exhibit dramatizes what could happen if we did not have reliable global positioning data. *Nauticus, Virginia.*

The cultural and natural traits of an area define the unique personality of a place. Sunset Crater Volcano National Monument, Arizona.

KARISSA DECARLO

KARISSA DECARLO

Timpanogos Cave National Monument, Utah.

Every Place has a Unique Personality.

The physical and human characteristics of a site give it meaning and set it apart from other places. A place's personality is defined by both the natural (plants, animals, geology) and cultural (land use, architecture, customs) traits of an area.

A term that is often used to refer to the personality of a place is setting. Think of your favorite book or movie. Chances are the author or director put a lot of effort into creating the setting – the place that frames the story. Knowing the details of a setting helps us conjure a mental image of a place and reveals its unique personality to us.

Bring to mind an image of your interpretive site. Pretend you are going to make a movie to tell the story of this place. How will you set the stage? Will you zoom in to a small area or pan out to a wide-angle view? How will you create vivid imagery – what sights, sounds, smells, tastes, and textures will you include? Painting a picture of the place where your story occurs will bring it to life for visitors.

Activity Ideas:

1) Write descriptions of easily recognizable landmarks and have visitors identify the places based on their unique characteristics.

2) Take visitors on a walk and ask them to point out and discuss the human and physical attributes of a place.

3) Ask participants to read or listen to a story about your site and then sketch the setting.

Trends in Place Interpretation

The meaning of place is arguably the most important theme in both geography and interpretation. Every place holds an extraordinary natural or cultural meaning—sometimes both. Interpreters strive to reveal the meaning of a place through carefully crafted programs and exhibits.

One goal of interpretation is to help visitors learn to appreciate places and inspire them to preserve both natural and cultural spaces. Yet sometimes our determination to preserve an interpretive site exactly as it is may leave people with a tenuous connection to a place. Our everyday lives are fraught with change, yet we often tell visitors that changes in our public lands are bad.

Place-based education specialist David Sobel warns that many of our traditional approaches to teaching people about place can inadvertently instill apathy and fear. Long lists of rules and prohibitions convey a hands-off approach to places, doom-and-gloom stories of climate change create a sense of hopelessness, and the needs of the people living in and near special places are frequently overlooked.

We need to carefully consider whether our traditional approaches to place interpretation are creating the strong bonds between people and places that we are striving to achieve.

How do we do this? We can start by examining certain trends that are emerging in the field of interpretation. These trends have the potential to transform our interpretive sites into *Yes Places, Hope Places,* and *People Places.*

Outdoor experiences help children learn to love the places we are trying to protect for their future enjoyment. *Bear Creek Nature Center, Colorado.*

Yes Places: Leaving No Child Inside

One of the first words children learn to say is "No". They learn this from the litany of *Nos* they hear from adults. *No, don't put that in your mouth. No, don't touch that. No, don't do that.*

The same is true of many of the public places that children visit. The entrance signs are frequently riddled with rules, regulations, prohibitions, and the many other ways we have found to say "No." A friend sent me this photo of an entrance kiosk she saw during a trip. The window is plastered with signs that say "No" followed by lists of prohibited activities. A child might rightly wonder—what can I do?

A new initiative, known as No Child Left Inside (NCLI), aims to change that. Based on the best-selling book by Richard Louv, *Last Child in the Woods*, this project encourages people to say "Yes" to children. *Yes, you can do that. Yes, you can explore that place. Yes, you can get really, really dirty.*

Louv shows the world the value of helping children connect with the great outdoors. He argues that nature lovers and nature defenders are born out of grubby hands and wet feet. Such

Rules and prohibitions convey a hands-off approach to places.

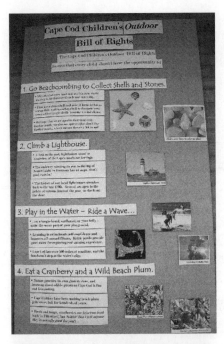

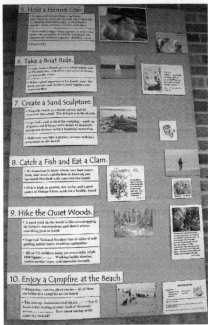

Cape Cod National Seashore posts a children's Outdoor Bill of Rights in the visitor center.

The interpretive playground at Fort Necessity National Battlefield, Pennsylvania.

experiences help children learn to love the places we are trying to protect for their future enjoyment.

A simple way for you to get involved in the NCLI movement is to find ways to say "Yes" to kids. Some places have taken on this challenge by developing a Children's Outdoor Bill of Rights. These rights include splashing in the water, camping under the stars, catching a fish, following a trail, and creating a sand sculpture.

An Outdoor Bill of Rights helps children discover what a specific place has to offer. While these rights may seem intuitive, people don't always exercise their rights unless they are encouraged to do so. This is important in a time where public land agencies are reporting a decline in the popularity of outdoor activities. Recent studies show that participation in outdoor recreation is down about 20 percent.

Cape Cod National Seashore posts a children's Outdoor Bill of Rights in its visitor center on a large, colorful display. A handout offers suggestions on how children can engage in the suggested activities. I encourage you to embrace this idea by asking yourself, *what do children have the right to do at my site?* Make "Yes" a more important word than "No" on your entrance signs and kiosks.

Other things you can do:

- Find ideas for getting kids outside at www.greenhour.com.

- Build an interpretive playground or outdoor discovery area. In 2007, the National Park Service unveiled its first interpretive playground at Fort Necessity National Battlefield. The play area is a miniature version of the interpretive site that allows children to explore the area at a scale that makes sense to them. Read more about this innovative approach to creating Yes Places at http://www.nps.gov/fone/parknews/playground.htm.

- Form a local No Child Left Inside initiative. The Children and Nature Network offers extensive ideas and resources. The group posts research studies, campaign activities, and community action guides on its website at www.childrenandnature.org.

- Advocate for legislation that supports the No Child Left Inside Act, which provides federal funding for environmental education and outdoor learning programs. For more information, visit www.nclicoalition.org.

Hope Places: Interpreting Climate Change

Geographer Dr. Joseph Kerski has this to say regarding the writing of a book called *Essentials of the Environment* (Kerski & Ross, 2005):

> It was easy to become discouraged after we examined the depleted fisheries, the logged rainforests, and the polluted ground water at a myriad of scales from local to regional. However, for every environmental issue, we made it a point to feature a story of a person, organization, or government agency making a positive difference. It turned out that these success stories weren't hard to find. Even if they didn't affect a large geographic area or a major amount of resources, they changed people's attitudes. This should give us hope for the future. Giving people information and experiences so they can make up their own minds is a fundamental goal of interpretation.

Awareness of human impacts on the Earth is critical. Climate change education is an important tool for dispelling misconceptions and fostering environmental consciousness. Yet educators and interpreters are starting to realize that telling people stories of catastrophic climate change is spurring apathy, not action.

The typical approach to interpreting climate change has all too often been: The Earth is like a greenhouse—you made it hotter by producing carbon dioxide when you drove your car here to read this sign—you are killing cute, cuddly baby polar bears—you need to go home and replace all of your light bulbs right now or we are all doomed.

Yet people who visit interpretive sites are on vacation or enjoying a day off. They want to be happy. "People don't want

HEIDI BAILEY

Did you know?
On November 27, 2008, a stick was inducted into the National Toy Hall of Fame. This time-honored toy takes its place beside Barbie, Slinky, Mr. Potato Head, Play-doh, and Teddy Bear. Visit www.childrenandnature. org/news/detail/stick_inducted_ into_toy_hall_of_fame for more information.

The Earth is Heating Up

What's the evidence?

Among climate scientists, there is little doubt that temperatures are rising. Our planet is hotter than it has been for thousands of years, and the pace of warming may be accelerating. The 1990s were hotter than any decade of the 20th century. 1998 the hottest year since instrumental record-keeping began in the late 1800s. As we enter the 21st century, this accelerated warming shows no signs of abating.

Vanishing Ice

The Earth is heating up, but not uniformly. In Alaska, for example, temperatures have risen at three times the global average in the last 30 years, melting permafrost, sea ice and land glaciers at unprecedented rates. Even in the relatively stable tropics, high altitude mountain glaciers are receding so quickly that many will disappear entirely within the next 15 years—an unmistakable sign that our climate is changing.

Do climate change exhibits and programs promote action or apathy? *Harvard University Museums, Massachusetts.*

to travel all the way from Florida to Mt. Rainier National Park to hear a lecture on water pollution" writes William J. Lewis in *Interpreting for Park Visitors*. "They've either heard it before or don't need the setting of Mt. Rainier to hear it now."

Interpretive sites are places for leisure and recreation, and they should capitalize on this fact by embracing the challenges we face as opportunities for innovation, joy, and discovery. Humans are not just a source of degradation and destruction; we are also an incredible resource of knowledge and creativity. We must help people discover the resources within themselves to bring about real innovation and change. Interpreters can do this by making visitors feel hopeful, not helpless.

Instead of taking the *world is burning up, go home and fix it right now* approach to interpreting climate change, let's give people information that inspires them to make changes instead of making them feel guilty. For instance, I enjoy reading about alternative energy technologies and ideas. I find stories about the individuals and companies that are stepping up to fund research and adopt greener practices fascinating and inspiring.

I think, "Wow—smart people are doing cool things to get us out of this mess. I want to be part of that. Show me more." Too often we just tell people which light bulb to buy because it is somehow better. Then they hear somewhere else a reason why the light bulb is bad—it releases mercury when broken. Then everyone is confused and they think, "Forget it."

In addition, many of the people participating in our programs— particularly children—may come from homes where the family is struggling to meet basic needs. In such cases, it is unfair to place the burden of our environment on families that can't afford to upgrade inefficient appliances and buy organically grown foods. Instead, let's help them see that they are part of a community that's working collectively towards a goal. Then perhaps someday—when their basic needs have been met—they can join in the fight to save our world as we know it.

Let's teach visitors about other people's efforts and allow them to decide when and how they want to participate. We know people like new technologies—thus the advent of interpretive podcasts and cell phone tours. Therefore, I propose replacing the static doomsday climate change exhibits with dynamic there-is-hope exhibits that focus on alternative technologies and lifestyles.

Climate change and alternative technologies are ever-changing subjects. Science is a process and anything to do with climate and weather is inexact and unpredictable. Let's try making exhibits that can be updated continuously as new research is revealed and others are proven or abandoned.

As an example, allow me to share some of the stories that I have read about in recent months. Many of these things seem like the stuff of science fiction today, but may become a reality in our future:

Energize Visitors with Energy Stories

Sun Savvy

Solar energy is a largely unexploited resource because solar panels are heavy, expensive, and less efficient than desired. But this is changing. New technology involves thermal solar (mirrors that focus heat to create steam), nanosolar (aluminum-foil thin sheets), solar concentrators (dye painted on window panes), solar fabrics, and solar-powered gadgets like flashlights and laptops. Keep track of sun savvy technology at http://www.greenoptimistic.com/category/solar-power/.

Weird Wind

You may have seen windmills standing like sentinels off the coast of a nearby beach. These turbines are mounted on the sea floor just like offshore oilrigs. But now, windmills are venturing into deeper waters atop floating platforms, and plans are underway to experiment with high-altitude flying turbines and wind sails. The corporate giant, Google, is funding research and development on high-altitude wind power and other technologies. Visit www.google.org.

H_2O to Go

Hydroelectric plants harness the power of rivers to create energy. Now ordinary H_2O is creating new opportunities for alternative energy: enhanced geothermal or "deep energy" comes from injecting water underground to absorb heat from inside the Earth; tidal turbines take advantage of the ebb and flow of tides; and osmotic power is generated by turning saltwater into freshwater. Keep track of these trends at: http://www.earthmagazine.org/earth/section/alternative_energy.

Biomimicry and Biofuels

Biomimicry is about copying nature's best ideas to create technologies that solve human problems. For instance, scientists are making solar collectors out of polyester textile that mimics the way a polar bear's hair collects heat. Other scientists are redesigning wind turbine blades with flipper bumps that mimic a humpback whale. Visit http://www.biomimicryinstitute.org/.

Biofuels generated from food resources like corn have proved to be controversial, but biofuels can also be generated from other sources—like pond scum. Biofuel created from algae is a truly green technology. Read more at http://www.earthmagazine.org/earth/article/1d6-7d9-2-d.

Stinky Solutions

Did you know that methane gas traps more than 20 times as much heat in the atmosphere as carbon dioxide? Methane gas is generated by waste from cows and landfills. Some farmers are starting to harness the power of methane by using "digesters" that extract methane from cow manure. Companies like SC Johnson are powering their plants using methane extracted from landfills: http://www.scjohnson.com/environment/conserving_10.asp. In China, some rural homes have biogas digesters that convert gas produced by human waste to household power.

Transition Towns

Many people feel that the job of eliminating our reliance on fossil fuels rests on the shoulders of scientists and politicians. But the new Transition Initiative empowers ordinary citizens to create changes at the community level. Learn more at: http://www.transitionus.org/.

Pedal Power

Generate energy when you work out! The Green Microgym harnesses human power to generate electricity http://thegreenmicrogym.com. A similar application is crowd farming, which uses special flooring blocks to capture kinetic energy from people when they walk, run, or dance.

Carbon-free TV

Ever watch the hit Fox TV show called 24? The show is now the first-ever carbon neutral television production. Visit http://gei.newscorp.com/.

Optimizing Optimism

I included the last two entries to show that if you look hard enough, you can find all sorts of interesting stories related to climate change. The more you can relate alternative energy to the daily lives of visitors, the greater your chance of making a connection. I encourage you to search for offbeat stories, explore the initiatives in your local area, and incorporate alternative technologies into the design of your visitor center. Here are a few resources:

- Search for stories at http://www.sundancechannel.com/ecommunity/#/ecommunityMap//.

- Read the book, *Earth the Sequel: The Race to Reinvent Energy* (W.W. Norton & Co.)

- Watch the films *Transforming Energy* (www.transformingenergy.com) or *Modern Marvels: Renewable Energy* (www.historychannel.com/minisites/modernmarvels).

- Take a look at *Get Energized*, an interactive program on energy education offered by the Bureau of Land Management: http://www.blm.gov/ca/st/en/prog/energy.html.

Stay current on alternative technologies by reading a monthly magazine like Earth (www.earthmagazine.org).

Visitors don't want to leave your interpretive site and chat about dying polar bears over pizza. But they might go away talking about the technologies and projects they learned about at your site. They might tell someone else about it, pay attention when they hear about it on the news, look it up on the internet, and maybe think, "There is hope—perhaps I can do something, too."

Does keeping up with such a dynamic subject seem like too much work? Try asking your staff and volunteers to pick a topic that interests them and track it. Invite local businesses and interest groups to provide information on their current projects. Once a month, or once a quarter, use this information to post an update—using interpretive techniques, of course—about each topic.

Here are some tips for turning your interpretive site into a Hope Place:

- Avoid portraying humans as the enemy. Stick to positive images.

- Focus less on global issues and technical information. Instead, focus on locally visible changes and observable effects on people's lives.

- Remember that visitors are inspired by personal experiences that connect them to places and by seeing other people making a difference.

Still not feeling energized? Watch the following episode of *Big Ideas for a Small Planet* at http://www.hulu.com/watch/15721/big-ideas-for-a-small-planet-power and hear a young girl's reaction to a demonstration of solar technology for homes:

> "It makes us feel really happy because we know there's hope now. It inspires people to also do other things, and if one person started, maybe a whole block or a whole neighborhood can end up getting involved."

So let's get started! What can you do to transform your interpretive site into a Hope Place?

THE FUTURE IS HOPEFUL

Transform your interpretive site into a Hope Place. *Cheyenne Mountain Zoo, Colorado.*

At the Lesvos Petrified Forest Geopark in Greece, the gift shop sells "taste boxes" that offer a sampling of local products.

Local women's cooperatives cater events hosted by the Geopark.

People Places: Sustaining Communities

In their book *Personal Interpretation*, authors Lisa Brochu and Tim Merriman share a few of their most memorable interpretive experiences, such as hiking and riding horseback with native guides and cooking tortillas with a local woman. These experiences didn't happen during a tour of an interpretive center, but out in the world during an informal encounter between people.

These types of experiences are at the heart of a new program known as the geopark initiative. At select sites throughout the world, local people and land managers are banding together to create an interpretive experience that focuses on Earth heritage and sustainable tourism. At the heart of this experience is a powerful resource—people.

The term geopark is the official designation of 58 places in 18 countries (see www.globalgeopark.org). A geopark is a partnership of people who share the job of protecting natural resources and interpreting the story of a place. A primary goal of a geopark is to encourage economic development by helping people improve their living conditions and the quality of their environment.

Geoparks accomplish this goal by reaching beyond the boundaries of protected areas to embrace local communities and small businesses. Geoparks create opportunities for local guides and service providers, offer local products, and promote interpretive experiences outside of park and recreation settings.

The geopark initiative is teaching the world a valuable lesson—local people are an important natural resource. Interpretive sites that use this resource with wisdom and respect are what I think of as People Places.

People Places do more than interpret and protect—they sustain. They sustain communities, economies, cultures, lifestyles, and families. Interpretive sites grow into People Places by deepening partnerships with neighboring towns, businesses, associations, and schools.

Mapping projects are an excellent way for communities to share their favorite places with visitors. Maps created by local people offer a diversity of viewpoints and a personalized portrayal of a place. The following are examples of maps made by young children, teenage students, and indigenous societies:

A map sign made by children in Manitou Springs, Colorado

Alexander County Mapbook
Students of a high school GIS class developed a map book of Alexander County in North Carolina. The book contains maps and information on all aspects of life, including arts, recreation, economics, history, and demographics. Read more at http://www.co.alexander. nc.us/index/achs-mapbook.php.

Native Maps
The Aboriginal Mapping Network creates maps that integrate georeferenced points, artwork, cultural memory, and other data. These maps portray a collective image of the culture of indigenous societies. Visit http://www.nativemaps.org/.

Alexander County Mapbook

Maps as Interpretive Tools

Garden of the Gods,
Colorado Springs,
Colorado.

"In viewing natural objects and scenes, the total amount we discern is nearly nothing compared to what there is to see…. And when it comes to understanding the why and how of what we do manage to see, which is vital to a feeling of its reality, we all need what help we can get."

—Freeman Tilden, *The National Parks*

Maps have the power to inspire the imagination and fuel curiosity about a place. A map can be a beautiful form of art, a window into another world, the path to a treasure, the secret to a mysterious place, or a fascinating storyteller.

Maps enable visitors to see areas that are too large to be viewed directly, leading them to understand, appreciate, and protect vast landscapes. Viewed in this light, maps are an extraordinary source of learning in interpretive settings.

Maps are also important for reaching visitors that don't attend educational programs, browse exhibits, or join interpretive walks. Many of these visitors will refer to a map during their stay to find out where they are, where they're going, and how to get there. A map may therefore be the only opportunity to communicate an interpretive message to certain visitors.

Frontline interpreters and guides are often responsible for orienting visitors to a site and communicating the meaning of a landscape. Yet staff training programs rarely devote any time to teaching map-reading skills even though they are needed on a daily basis. This chapter covers the basics of using maps in interpretive settings to connect visitors with places.

Don't worry—a compass is not required.

What is a Map?

A map is a picture of the world around us. A map can show the inside of a human cell or an entire galaxy. A map can be a picture of a real place or an imagined one. A map can be intended strictly for business or can be a beautiful form of art. Maps can be funny or serious, static or animated, flat or three-dimensional, black and white or color. A map can be hand-drawn, computer-generated, or layered over a photograph.

Maps can be abstract or very realistic. A map can be small enough to put in your pocket or large enough to walk through. A map can be drawn by a child or developed by a professional cartographer. Many maps exist only in our minds—we use these mental maps to find our way to work or school. Maps are as varied as the people who use them, yet all maps have some basic characteristics in common.

A map is a picture made up of dots, lines, and shapes that represent landmarks, roads, and large areas of land. Geographers call these elements point, line, and area features. In this book, I refer to them as places, paths, and patterns—the three Ps. These elements are the parts of a map. Together they create a meaningful whole.

A map is only as meaningful as the physical landscape it represents. Freeman Tilden said, "Interpretation should aim to present a whole rather than a part." The purpose of learning to read the parts of a map is to understand the meaning of a whole—a whole map, a whole place, a whole landscape.

A Map is like a Droodle

Learning to find the hidden meaning in a map is a lot like trying to solve a riddle. A map is similar to a specific type of riddle called a droodle. A droodle—or doodle riddle—is a picture made up of dots, lines, and shapes that doesn't make sense unless you are given a clue. Like most riddles, people create them as fun and challenging puzzles for others to solve.

Maps enable visitors to see areas that are too large to be viewed directly. *Petroglyph National Monument, New Mexico.*

Maps can lead visitors to understand, appreciate, and protect vast landscapes. *Bureau of Land Management.*

Can you guess the meaning of these droodles? Find the answers to these droodles at the end of this chapter.

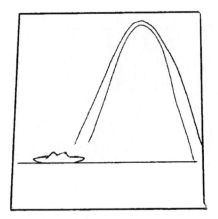

A map is like a droodle—it's a picture made up of dots, lines, and shapes that only makes sense when people are given clues to its meaning. Both droodles and maps are an abstraction of reality. Maps give clues to their meaning by using color, symbols, scales, and legends. People must learn to interpret these clues before they can decipher a map. The ability to derive meaning from a map is part of a person's spatial knowledge.

Spatial Knowledge

People possess many different types of knowledge. Mathematical knowledge involves understanding numbers, quantities, and logic. Verbal knowledge applies to letters, sounds, words, and meanings. Musical knowledge relates to tones, rhythms, and melodies. Spatial knowledge involves mental rotation, remembering routes, understanding scale, and visualizing a three-dimensional environment.

We all have an innate ability to visualize an unseen place, imagine traveling along a route, and rotate mental imagery to look at an area from a different point of view. This ability allows us to remember landmarks, find our way home, and see patterns in a landscape. Interpretation has the power to reveal the meaning of a place by encouraging people to visualize the three Ps: places, paths, and patterns.

Geographers study how people learn about the space around them and how they gain knowledge from maps. Think about the last time you visited a new city. You most likely identified a few key locations first—the airport, hotel, conference center, pub, etc.—and then you figured out the routes you needed to take to travel from one place to another. You would have needed to stay a while before you learned the layout of the city well enough to give directions or devise shortcuts.

People go through three steps when they are learning their way around a new place. Geographers call these steps landmark knowledge, route knowledge, and survey knowledge:

Landmark knowledge relates to a person's ability to describe what a location is, along with its associated meaning or significance.

Route knowledge relates to a person's ability to determine how far and in which direction to travel to move between significant locations.

Survey knowledge relates to a person's understanding of the layout of an area and of spatial patterns and relationships.

Have you ever had to return to a known point—such as a hotel—to find your way to another place? What level of spatial knowledge had you achieved? Most visitors' concepts of a landscape is limited to the road; people don't stay in a place long enough to move beyond route knowledge.

Interpretation can help visitors go through the three-step spatial learning process faster. And once visitors feel oriented and comfortable in a new environment, they will have more time to form a personal connection with a place.

Maps Through the Ages

Map use is a learned skill much like reading or math. The ability of a five-year-old to understand maps will be very different from that of an adult. Author David Sobel, who specializes in using maps for place-based education, identified four distinct stages in map learning in his book, *Map Making with Children: Sense of Place Education for the Elementary Years:*

Age 5–6: Maps that focus on the immediate surroundings—on what children can see and experience directly—are appropriate at this age. Young children tend to visualize their world from a frontal view rather than a bird's-eye view. Therefore, maps should look more like pictures, murals, or three-dimensional models.

Age 7–8: At this age, children can visualize slightly larger areas such as a city block or a campground. Children will begin to include partial pathways when they draw maps—perhaps a sidewalk or the trail to the visitor center. At this age, children begin to visualize their world from a slightly higher perspective—as if they are looking out a second story window. Take a look at the maps in many popular children's books. The illustrators typically draw these maps from a slightly elevated perspective.

Age 9–10: Children can now comprehend larger areas such as communities and watersheds. They can connect paths into networks and understand more abstract concepts such as map scale. At this point, children can visualize areas as a combination of frontal and bird's-eye views. Panoramic maps that simulate overlooking an area from a high vantage point, such as a hill, are appropriate. Tourist maps are often designed in this manner since many adults retain a preference for this type of map.

Age 11 and up: Starting around this age, people can comprehend regional and world geography. They can fully develop map-

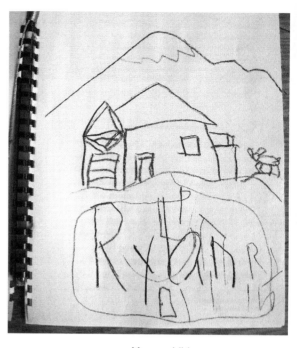

Young children visualize their world from a frontal view rather than a bird's-eye view. *Pikes Peak Heritage Center, Colorado.*

Tourist maps are often panoramic since many adults retain a preference for this type of map. *Empire State Building, New York.*

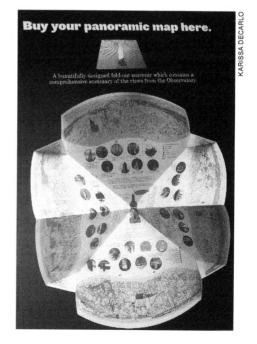

KARISSA DECARLO

reading skills and learn to navigate with maps. The ability to visualize an area from a bird's-eye or aerial view also emerges. However, just as reading level and mathematical ability varies widely among people, the map sophistication of visitors will be vastly different.

When designing map exhibits and programs, interpreters should always consider the audience. Aerial maps and images may not be well understood by all people. Therefore, models, murals, pictorial maps, and panoramic images may be more readily understood by the greatest number of visitors.

In addition, most people find it easier to relate to nearby places than to far-away spaces. Thus, maps that focus on nearby places should provide the starting point for most programs and exhibits. Begin by zooming into a local area and then panning out to a regional or global view.

Cracking the Map Code

Visitors may be unpracticed in decoding map clues. Interpretation can help visitors develop their map-reading skills and increase their level of spatial knowledge. This can be accomplished through activities that involve maps. You can choose from two types of activities depending on your objectives: affective (emotional) map activities and cognitive (intellectual) map activities.

Affective activities help visitors connect to the meaning or significance of a place. Rather than focusing on map accuracy, these activities are intended to help visitors develop a sense of place. For example, participants might create a map collage of an area with bark rubbings, pinecones, pebbles, and other materials they find.

Cognitive activities are best for site orientation and navigation. Map skills activities help visitors understand scale, symbols, distance, direction, and the relative location of places. The next section provides an overview of map skills and a sample activity for each.

Sense of Place Mapping Exercise

Sound Map
Ask each participant to draw a symbol of him or her self in the middle of an 8.5-by-11-inch sheet of paper. Invite everyone to find a comfortable place to sit for a time without talking. Encourage the participants to open their senses and listen closely to their surroundings. Ask them to map the sounds they hear in relation to where they are sitting.

Super-Sonic Sound Map
After completing the above activity, ask participants to turn the sheet of paper over and start again. This time, tell them to pretend they have a super power that allows them to hear things that other people can't hear. Encourage them to look around them and imagine they can hear the sound of a spider spinning its web, electricity coursing through the walls, or a plant growing. Ask them to map these "super-sonic" sounds in relation to where they are sitting. At the end of the activity, see if anyone would like to share his or her map with the group.

Decoding Map Clues

Compass Rose

A compass rose is a map clue that lets you know which way you are going. Most maps that show large areas of the Earth such as cities, states, and countries are oriented with north at the top. But maps of smaller areas such as interpretive trails are sometimes oriented to the local landscape. In this case, the map may show south, west, east, or someplace in between at the top. Always look for the compass rose or directional arrow for a clue to how a map is drawn.

Scale

Map scale is a clue that allows you to see how the size of a map compares to the size of the Earth. Map scales come in three different varieties. A ratio scale uses the same units to compare the distance on a map to a distance on the ground. For instance 1:24,000 means that one inch on a map equals 24,000 inches on the ground. Since 24,000 inches (2,000 feet) is difficult to visualize, the second type of scale—a verbal scale—uses more familiar units, such as one inch equals one mile.

The third, and probably the most useful, type of map scale is a bar scale. This type of scale allows you to measure a distance on a map using a piece of paper or a string and then physically compare it to the bar scale. A bar scale is the best type of map scale to use. If a map is reduced or enlarged, the scale will still be accurate. With a ratio or verbal scale, changing the size of the map will mean that one inch will no longer equal the same distance on the ground.

To measure the distance from one place to another, mark the distance on a scrap of paper and compare it to the bar scale at the bottom of the map. If a route

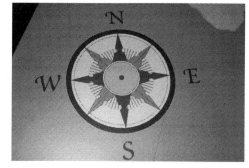

A compass rose offers a clue to which way a map is oriented. *Nauticus, Virginia.*

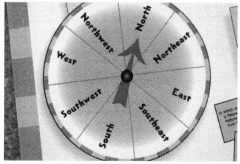

Have visitors pick a direction by twirling a spinner attached to a compass rose. Ask them where they would be headed if they set off from the visitor center in that direction. Find more maptivity ideas in Great Map Games, Scholastic, Inc.

Scale is a clue that allows you to see how the size of a model compares to the size of the real thing.

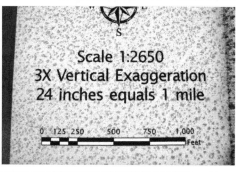

Map scales come in three varieties: ratio, verbal, and bar scales. *Mesilla Valley Bosque State Park, New Mexico.*

Provide a scrap of paper or attach a bar scale "ruler" to a map with a cord and invite visitors to figure out the distances between places. A long cord marked with scale increments can be used to measure curvy paths. *Florissant Fossil Beds National Monument, Colorado.*

involves changes in direction, move the piece of paper and mark each segment one at a time. If the route is curvy, lay a string along the entire distance and mark the endpoint with a thumb and forefinger. Compare this section of string to the bar scale.

Symbols and Legends

A symbol is a picture that shows where things are. Maps have three types of symbols: point, line, and area. These symbols correspond to the three Ps— places, paths, and patterns.

The features represented by symbols on a map depend on how zoomed in the map is. For instance, point symbols on a map of the U.S. will represent large cities or national parks. Points on a map of your site may represent individual buildings or exhibit areas. A point symbol may be a dot, a pictogram, or even a three-dimensional drawing. In general, the less abstract a symbol is, the easier it will be for people to understand.

Standard road and topographic maps use a lot of symbols. In this case map readers need a key or legend to help them decipher their meanings. A legend is a chart that explains the meaning of the symbols on a map. Since visitors are usually short on time, legends on visitor maps should be short. Maps that use colors, pictures, and labels effectively can eliminate the need for numerous symbols and a long legend.

Projections

Next time you peel an orange, try to take the peel off in on piece and then flatten it. What happens? The peel will tear in some places and buckle in others. Mapmakers have this same problem when they try to turn a globe into a map. A globe is round; a map is rectangular.

A map symbol is a picture that shows where things are. *Boston Children's Museum, Massachusetts.*

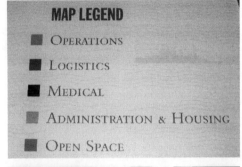

A legend is a chart that explains the meaning of symbols on a map. *Nauticus, Virginia.*

Create BINGO cards with different arrangements of map symbol pictures. Read off the names of symbols randomly until someone fills a row, column, or diagonal on the BINGO card. Find instructions for this activity at: http:// edcommunity.esri. com/arclessons/ lesson.cfm?id=425.

Imagine taking a photo of your face—which is roughly round—and turning it into a square. You would have to stretch out your forehead and chin a lot and your eyes and mouth a little—the only things that would look normal would be your nose and your ears.

Most of the world maps that hung on the walls of our classrooms when we were growing up looked like this. As a result, most of us grew up thinking that South America is smaller than Greenland, when it is actually more than eight times larger. The northern continents on these maps tend to be exaggerated in size relative to the continents in the south. Some say the stretching of the continents gives northerners a stretched ego, too.

In response to this, a man named Peters made a map that more accurately portrays area. This map puts all of us back in our place, but it gives the continents a bit of a squished look.

All of these flat maps of the Earth are called projections. Imagine putting a light in the center of a globe and projecting it onto a wall. You would need a round room to see everything on the Earth at the right size and shape. To make the image flat, you would have to peel the projection away like the orange peel and lay it out flat. To keep the map from tearing, some parts of the map would have to be distorted.

A flat map of the Earth may therefore show true direction, true distance, true area, or true shape, but never all four. On the map that hung on your classroom wall, direction was true, while on the Peters map, area is true. Another projection, the Robinson map, is becoming increasingly popular because it provides a better balance between the two.

Why are projections important? If you are comparing the habitat areas of different animals throughout the world,

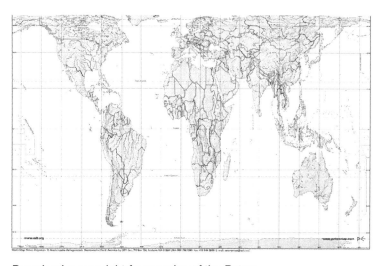

Download a copyright-free version of the Peters Map Projection at http://www.odtmaps.com/free_maps/peters-map-free-prints.asp.

The Robinson Map Projection offers the best balance between size and shape. Download a free Robinson projection – suitable for a 6-feet wide poster – at http://www.shadedrelief.com/natural/pages/download.html. *Lesvos Petrified Forest Museum, Greece.*

KATARZYNA KOZINA

KARISSA DECARLO

Above: *St. Louis Zoo, Missouri.*
Above, right: *Nauticus, Virginia.*
Right: *Florissant Fossil Beds.*

This world map is marked with a geographic coordinate grid. *Meteor Crater National Park, Arizona.*

KARISSA DECARLO

you will need a map that shows true area. If you want to figure out how far apart two places are, you want a map that shows true distance. A real globe is often the best choice because it represents true direction, distance, area, and shape. If you need to use a flat map, do a little research to see which projection will best serve your needs.

Grids

The town or city where you live uses street names and house numbers or building and apartment numbers to create a unique address for you and your neighbors. Geographers found a way to create a unique address for every place on the Earth by using a grid system.

Open your phone book to the map section and you will find a list of streets printed alongside a letter and number designator. The letters and numbers form a grid of columns and rows that allows you to locate a specific street. Can you find your street on the map? Which grid square is it in?

The Earth's grid system is called the Geographic Coordinate Grid. This system uses latitude and longitude to help you locate a specific place on the surface of the Earth. Lines of latitude start at the equator—the invisible belt that wraps around the Earth's waist. Lines of latitude are parallel to the equator and lines of longitude are perpendicular to the Equator.

Instead of using a letter and number like your phone book, latitude and longitude are written in degrees, minutes, and seconds. Don't be misled—these minutes and seconds have nothing to do with time. Here is an example: N 38°44'37" W109°29'58". This is the address for the Delicate Arch at Arches National Park.

Do you know the geographic address of your interpretive site?

Visitors can practice using map grids by playing a Battleship-style game. Create identical map grids on opposing tables. Ask visitors to place props on the maps and take turns guessing which grid squares contain props on the opposing side. *Boston Museum of Science, Massachusetts.*

Delicate Arch, Arches National Park, Utah.

Contour Lines

Contour lines connect the dots between points on the landscape that are at the same elevation. If the lines are close together, the terrain is steep, if they are far apart, the terrain is gentle.

Contours (A) always point downhill except where there is a stream or gully. In this case, the contours point upstream and appear v-shaped.

A contour interval (B) is the change in elevation from one contour to another, for instance 40 feet. If you walked along a contour line you would stay perfectly level, but if you walked from one line to another, you would go up or down 40 feet.

Thicker contour lines with numbers (C) are called index contours. You can find the elevation of other contour lines by adding or subtracting the amount of the contour interval.

A circle of contour lines with hash marks pointing inward (D) indicates a depression or hole in the ground.

Circles without hash marks (E) are the peaks of hills or mountains. They will often have an X indicating a spot elevation.

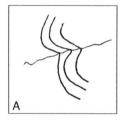

A

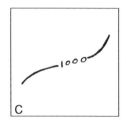

C

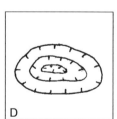

D

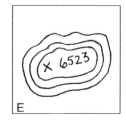

E

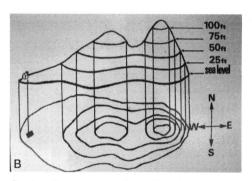

B

Contour lines connect the dots between points on the landscape that are at the same elevation.

Use stackable foam contours to draw a contour map.

Don't have foam cutouts? Use a potato.

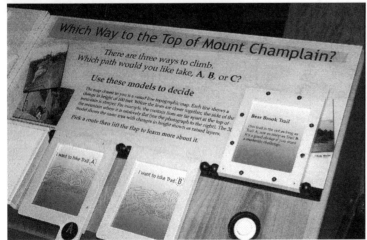

Ask visitors to pick a hiking trail based on a contour map. *Boston Museum of Science, Massachusetts.*

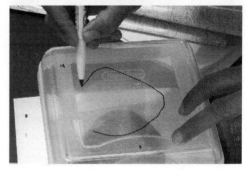

Place a stone "mountain" in a plastic box with a clear lid. Pour a small amount of water into the box and trace the shoreline onto the lid with a washable marker. Continue filling and drawing until the stone is submerged.

Types of Visitor Maps

Here is a list of the types of maps commonly found in interpretive settings:

Road and Trail Maps—Visitors use these maps to plan out travel routes along roads and trails. These maps typically offer detailed information on the distance between points, the locations of intersections, and the availability of facilities.

Topographic Maps—These maps use wavy lines known as contours to represent the physical shape of the landscape. A topographic map shows visitors the details of the terrain such as cliffs, hills, streams, and valleys.

Tourist Maps—These maps are graphical destination guides that introduce visitors to the amenities of a place such as tourist attractions, restaurants, hotels, and shops. Tourist maps are often commercial products that contain advertisements. They may be cartoon-like in appearance.

Floor Plans—Maps of the interior of museums, interpretive centers, and other buildings are known as floor plans. These maps show the location and size of rooms, walls, corridors, and exhibit areas.

Map of shuttle routes at Grand Canyon National Park, Arizona.

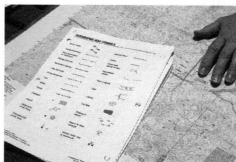

Topographic map symbols represent landscape features.

Tourist map of Durango, Colorado, by www. discoverymap.com.

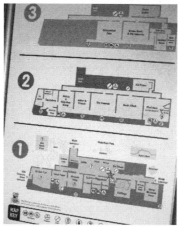

Floor plan for the Boston Children's Museum, Massachusetts.

Photo image map with trail overlay. *Mesilla Valley Bosque State Park, New Mexico.*

Data map of the WWII Battle of the Atlantic. Symbols show the locations of ships that sunk between 1942 and 1943. *Nauticus, Virginia.*

Interpretive map brochure of Hawaii Volcanoes National Park.

Droodle answers: Smokey Bear at Jefferson Expansion Memorial (left). Hiker watching rafters at Grand Canyon National Park (right).

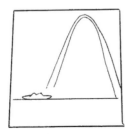

Photo Image Maps—Some maps are created from aerial photographs or satellite images of an area. These maps may have graphical symbols and labels superimposed over the images to help visitors identify landscape features.

Information or Data Maps—These maps focus on a specific subject such as geologic formations, population statistics, or economic data. Information maps represent data using a combination of color codes, symbols, and map keys (legends).

Interpretive Maps—These maps are designed to foster a sense of place or to convey a theme or message. Interpretive maps employ visualization techniques such as shaded relief, artistic renderings, and computer-generated scenes to provide a more realistic image of the landscape.

Map labels visible:
HALEAKALĀ NATIONAL PARK
Haleakalā Visitor Center
Park Headquarters Visitor Center
YOU ARE HERE
PACIFIC OCEAN
ISLAND OF MAUI
Kahului Airport
Kahului Bay
Ma'alaea Bay
West Maui Mountains

5

NATIONAL PARK SERVICE

Planning Interpretive Maps

"Try to make your maps evocative of the landscape in your park. Try to create a sense of place on paper, because a map is not only a sign but a metaphor."

—Megan Kealy, *Mapmaking for Parklands*

Above: *Haleakala National Park.*

A map can do so much more than show visitors the location of the restrooms. Maps can help people identify with large spaces, recognize patterns in the landscape, and find meaning in broader environments.

Well-designed interpretive maps can encourage visitors to explore a place and inspire them to support its conservation. Just as exhibits and signs play a role in the overall strategic plan of a park, maps can and should be used to play a similar interpretive role.

Various surveys have found that approximately 60 percent of museum visitors use hand-held maps, over 75 percent of people on a long day hike carry a map, and about 90 percent of National Park visitors use map brochures. By comparison, only 25 percent of National Park visitors use exhibits and less than 10 percent attend

Heidi Bailey **47**

People visiting unfamiliar environments need maps. *Grand Canyon National Park. Arizona.*

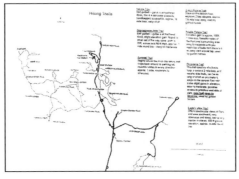

Many maps require visitors to fill in too many details to form a clear picture of the landscape.

ranger-led talks.

People visiting unfamiliar environments need maps—they don't necessarily need exhibits or programs. Yet few maps are designed as stand-alone interpretive products. They may be placed within or near interpretive media, but the map itself is rarely designed according to the principles of interpretation.

If you were designing an exhibit about a squirrel, you wouldn't provide a dot-to-dot picture or rough sketch of a squirrel. You would use a full-color photo or model that shows details such as the texture of fur, the size of the teeth, and perhaps the squirrel's home, food preferences, and habitat. Many maps are like the dot-to-dot picture or rough sketch—visitors have to fill in too many details to form a clear picture of the landscape.

This chapter is intended to help interpretive sites reach more visitors by learning to create better interpretive maps. The six-step process outlined in this chapter provides a simple method for planning maps that effectively orient visitors and connect them to the meaning of a place.

Getting Ready to Plan

Before you start planning your map, there are a number of questions you should ask yourself:

Do you really need a map?
Depending on the subject you are interpreting, a map may not always be the best solution. For orientation purposes, written directions may be more effective in telling visitors which way to go. For interpretation purposes, other types of graphical depictions may be more effective at conveying your theme or message. Consider the penguin sign images on the next page.

What is the purpose of your map?
Maps can serve many different purposes. Decide if your map is meant to serve as an orientation tool, destination guide, or interpretive media. Avoid using one map for all of these purposes. Like an exhibit or program, visitor maps should be clear, concise, and easy to understand. Too much information will clutter your map. If you have multiple reasons for making a map, you may need to create more than one.

Who is the audience?
Determine who will use your map. Will people be using your map at home to plan their trip? Is the map intended for hiking, driving, or exploring an exhibit area? Will your map be viewed on a wayside sign or as part of an interpretive exhibit? Different map users have different needs and map-reading abilities. As with any interpretive media, knowing your audience will help you plan and design more user-friendly maps.

What geographic area will you focus on?
Choose the amount of physical space that you want to depict on your map. Do you need to focus on the inside of a building, an interpretive loop, an entire system of hiking trails, a habitat area, a battlefield, or the whole park? Knowing the geographic area you need to focus on will help you determine the size and scale of your map.

Where will your map be displayed?
Select the place(s) your map will be displayed or distributed. Will the map be on the internet, in a brochure, at a trailhead, or inside an interpretive center? Modern map-making tools allow you to produce maps in multiple formats (electronic, print, raised relief) using the same data.

These three exhibits convey the same message: many kinds of penguins live in many places. The maps are the focus of the first two exhibits, but the penguins take center stage on the third exhibit. Always consider if a map is the best way to communicate your theme or message. From top to bottom: *Cheyenne Mountain Zoo, Colorado; St. Louis Zoo, Missouri; Wichita Zoo, Kansas.*

Knowing your audience will help you plan and design better maps. *Corps of Discovery II.*

Six Steps to Better Interpretive Maps

Step 1: Theme

Before you design, have a theme in mind. Every sign, exhibit, and program has a thematic title—why not maps? Tell visitors what is special about the space represented by your map. How are all of the places on your map related? What is the meaning of the landscape?

Visitors use maps to decide what they want to see, figure out which way to go, and obtain an overall image of an area. If a map is thematic, visitors can learn a little something, too.

A map can convey a message or theme similar to an exhibit or interpretive program. The space portrayed by a map has meanings that may not be readily evident to visitors. This meaning may be natural, historical, or cultural.

A thematic title can connect visitors to the meaning of the real-world space that a map represents. Developing a map theme can also determine what area is to be mapped, clarify the purpose of the map, and identify the intended audience.

Developing a theme for a map may seem daunting at first, but the theme may present itself naturally after a series of questions are answered. The answers to many of these questions are probably already being interpreted by other means. Thus, the geographic story can be easily incorporated into existing programs and exhibits.

Developing a Theme

Read through the questions below and think about how they apply to your site. Record your thoughts on a piece of scrap paper. Use your answers to develop a theme for a map of your site.

- What is the significance of the area that is to be mapped?

- How have the individual places and paths interacted over time?

- Why should visitors want to explore this space?

- Was this space created by a certain phenomenon?

- Does this space provide the context for an event?

- How does this space relate to the daily lives of visitors?

- How does the meaning at this scale differ from other scales?

- Does the arrangement of landscape features influence human or natural processes?

- What would be different if this space was altered?

- Has this space always appeared as it does today?

- Why is it important to protect this space?

The meaning of a landscape may not be evident to visitors. *Mount St. Helens National Volcanic Monument, Washington.*

Step 2: Levels of Information

A map with too much information is like a sign with too much text. An effective exhibit breaks information down into small, easily digestible pieces. These pieces represent different levels, or components, of an exhibit. Maps can also be broken down into smaller chunks that are easier for visitors to process.

In Chapter 4, we learned that maps are made up of places, paths, and patterns (points, lines, and areas). You can use these three levels of information to break maps into smaller chunks of information as follows:

Places—Describe significant landmarks, features, and other points of interest

Paths—Highlight routes or the paths of humans, animals, plants, water, wind, ice, products, ideas

Patterns—Emphasize important relationships, the layout of an area, or landscape patterns

Start by showing the locations of important places, then add paths or routes of movement, and finally show how these places interact to create a spatial pattern. Layer these maps or place them side-by-side.

Let's consider a few examples:

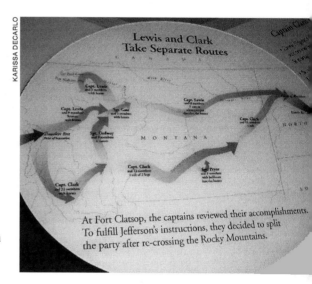

This map highlights the routes traveled by Lewis & Clark on their journey home. *Lewis & Clark National Historic Interpretive Center, Montana.*

- You want to use a map to show the habitat for an animal. You could highlight the habitat area on a single map, or you could use a series of maps to interpret your subject. Start with a map that highlights significant features, such as a grove of trees used for shelter, a meadow used for feeding, a rock formation used for dens, and so on. On the second map, highlight the animals' movement during a 24-hour period or over the course of a year. On the third map, show how this habitat is connected to similar areas, creating a habitat corridor.

- You want to use a map to interpret a battle. On the first map, highlight landforms, forts, and other features that were important during the battle. On the second map, show the paths of troop movements. On the final map, show the outcome of the battle—a hill that was taken, a fort that fell, the territory captured by the victors.

- You want to use a map to interpret a fire regime. On the first map, highlight familiar features that will orient visitors. Add a second map layer that shows the path of an ancient fire as indicated by fire-scarred trees. Add a third layer that shows recent fire activity. Can your visitors identify a pattern?

Maps, either handheld or much larger, like this one at Governor Mike Huckabee Delta Rivers Nature Center in Pine Bluff, Arkansas, are essential to a positive visitor experience.

A Note about Patterns

This level of information is the one that interpretive maps, and therefore visitors, usually miss. Below are some tips for focusing on patterns.

The various forces of history, the Earth, and human development conspired to make your interpretive site a special place. Think about what the area as a whole means to you. What could you share with others about this space? Look at a map of your site—what patterns exist that visitors may not see? Ask yourself the following questions:

- Did the lay of the land contribute to the outcome of a battle?

- Were the conditions just right for a rare species to thrive?

- Was your site the perfect place for native peoples to settle?

- Were natural processes responsible for creating a scenic jewel?

- Did citizens preserve or create a special place within an urban area?

- Even the floor plan of a building can have a pattern. Is your building or exhibit area laid out by shape, topic, chronology, or region?

Step 3: Type of Map

Maps are miniature representations of the world around us. Space can be represented in a multitude of ways and planners must first determine the type of spatial representation that is desired. A flat map will offer a two-dimensional representation of a place. A topographic model will provide a three-dimensional representation of a space. An animation can include both the dimensions of space and time. The type of map you choose will depend on the story you wish to convey, where the map will be displayed, and the amount of money you can spend.

In addition to the dimensionality of the map, you must also determine the size, point of view, and orientation of your map.

Map Size

Make your map bigger. Increasing the size of the map or display used to communicate spatial knowledge can help visitors perceive large landscapes. Visitors have to mentally transform every map into the large landscape it represents. The larger the map, the easier it is for visitors to relate it to the real world.

Many brochure maps are so small that they make it difficult for visitors to visualize large areas. Visitors need maps that are transportable and easy to fold, yet many brochure maps have plenty of room for expansion. Often, the size of a large landscape is reduced to as small as two by two inches. This increases the difficulty of mentally transforming the map into the real place it represents.

I am often asked exactly how big maps should be. The truth is, there is no standard size that fits all situations. You will need to consider the needs of your visitors on a case-by-case basis. If your map will be used as part of a driving tour, it should fit comfortably in your visitor's lap. If your map will be used outside and it tends to be windy, your map should be small enough not to flap in the wind. Make a few mock-ups of your map using scrap paper and see which size works best for your situation. Your map should be as large as possible while still providing a comfortable map-reading experience for your visitors.

Exhibit maps have the advantage of not needing to fit into a visitor's pocket. Wall- or room-size displays are often better suited to helping people understand the geography of an area. Larger maps enable visitors to immerse themselves in a space and travel vicariously through a landscape.

Point of View

Most maps use a bird's-eye view to represent the landscape—we are not birds! An oblique (slanting) view of buildings and landforms can provide a more realistic effect. Research indicates that people prefer an oblique view of 45–60 degrees.

Oblique or panoramic maps are more effective because they simulate a three-dimensional view of an area and are more comfortable and engaging for visitors. Ski areas commonly use these types of maps because the panoramic views of the lifts and runs on a mountain are easy for visitors to understand.

In a study conducted at Zion National Park (http://www.nps.gov/hfc/carto/ zion_map_study.pdf), researchers found that three-dimensional maps attract more visitors and hold their attention longer. They are also better for helping people to identify their position in space, comprehend the distance between places, and visualize the physical shape of the landscape. Three-dimensional maps are particularly well suited for areas of high topographic relief. They provide a clear picture of the amount of effort required to

Larger maps are easier for visitors to relate to the real world. *Columbia River Gorge National Scenic Area, Oregon.*

Room-size maps enable visitors to travel vicariously through a large landscape. *Missouri River Interpretive Center, Nebraska.*

Panoramic views of ski areas are easy for visitors to understand. *Canada Olympic Park, Calgary.*

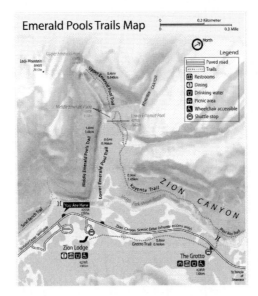
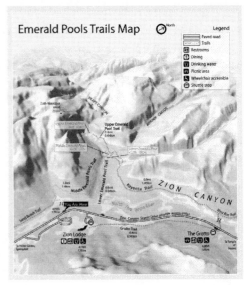

Compare the two-dimensional map on the left with the three-dimensional map on the right. Which do you think provides a clearer picture of the landscape? *Zion National Park, Utah. National Park Service.*

traverse the terrain. Be aware that these maps distort scale and are not intended for precise navigation.

If your budget does not allow for a three-dimensional map, you may want to add an elevation profile to maps. This is an important safety consideration, as visitors may underestimate the difficulty of a hiking trail portrayed by a two-dimensional map. Certain software packages (see http://www.natgeomaps.com/) allow you to create and print elevation profiles for trails and backcountry routes.

Map Orientation

A map's orientation denotes whether it is aligned to a local setting or a global coordinate system. In general, maps that are aligned with the local terrain are easier for visitors to use. Often, an interpretive site produces a map and uses it throughout the site without consideration of the map's orientation relative to the local terrain.

The Earth is round—north does not have to be at the top of your map. The word orient has traditionally been associated with the east and the direction of the rising sun. For centuries, many maps were *orient*-ed with east at the top. Similarly, early maps of the continent of Africa placed south at the top. These historical maps reflect the values and perspective of the cultures that created them.

Taking a lesson from history, certain maps should reflect the perspective of visitors by being aligned to the local setting. Since people associate the top part of a map with forward movement, placing the location of visitor centers or other entrance points at the bottom of a map invites visitors to venture forth into the landscape.

This map is oriented to the south. The "You Are Here" symbol at the bottom of the map invites visitors to venture forth into the landscape. *Red Rock Canyon Open Space, Colorado.*

Interpretive map designers should take into consideration the alignment of the visitor to the landscape when they view the map. Where is the visitor most likely to pick up the map and enter the landscape? Put this location at the bottom.

This technique does not apply to all visitor maps. Drivers with road maps and hikers with topo maps may be confused if visitor maps are not oriented with North at the top. The decision on how to orient a map should be made on a case-by-case basis. Here are some guidelines:

North at the Top

- Map depicts a large geographic area

- Map is distributed in multiple locations

- Map is likely to be cross-referenced with a road or topographic map

Aligned with Local Terrain

- Map depicts a small geographic area

- Map is used at one location or entry point

- Most map features can be seen from where the visitor is standing

Step 4: Visuals

This step involves planning the content of a map and how it will be portrayed. Start by making a list of the features that you want to include. Be selective, but don't omit important geographic information. The decisions you have made up to this point—about the map's purpose, audience, theme, and levels of information—will help you decide which features to include.

After you compile your list, rank the features in order of importance. In Chapter 6, you will learn different design techniques that allow you to accentuate certain features and subdue others. Once you have created an ordered list, write down next to each item how the feature will be portrayed (symbolically or realistically) and identified (with labels or a legend).

If your budget allows for a more sophisticated map, you may want to consider opting for a map that uses realism rather than symbolism. The National Park Service's approach to designing visitor maps uses artistically inspired maps to offer a stylized view of the Earth (see "Getting Real: Reflecting on the New Look of National Park Service Maps" at the end of this chapter).

Here are some ways to create more realistic maps:

- Add color and shaded relief to create maps that mimic the look and feel of the landscape. For information on shaded relief, visit www.shadedrelief.com.

- Replace abstract map symbols with drawings or photos. A drawing in the shape of a tree, pond, or building is more enticing than a dot.

- Create an artistic rendering of the area by overlaying map features onto a landscape style painting, an aerial photograph, or a satellite image.

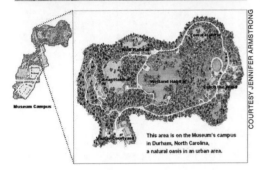

KARISSA DECARLO

Top: In this model, the floor of the Grand Canyon is depicted in shaded relief. *Canyon View Visitor Center, Arizona.*

Middle: *Museum of Life and Science, North Carolina.*

Immediately above: *Mount St. Helen's National Park, Washington.*

Step 5: Text

Use words to describe something interesting about your map. A verbal description can guide visitors to the stories hidden within maps and the landscapes they represent.

Text focuses the visitor's attention on specific elements within the map and relates a story about these elements. In addition, text supports the double encoding of spatial knowledge, which occurs when people store information both verbally and visually.

Map text should do three things:

1. Invite visitors to look at the map.

2. Tell visitors what the map shows.

3. Explain why this pattern is important.

For example, the text below the map on the Bayou Salado sign points out a pattern in the landscape and explains its significance:

> Colorado's four mountain parks, visible from space, are high-elevation prairies that serve as transition zones for many plant and animal species.

When telling visitors what a map shows, avoid jumping all over the place. Map descriptions that mimic reading a page in a book (left to right, top to bottom) will generally be easier for visitors to follow. Consider the text to the right of the map:

> Mountains ring the basin. The unique rock formations to the *east* are part of the Kenosha and Tarryall Mountains. The Mosquito Range lies to the *west* and the Park Range is on the *north*.... In the *south* are the volcanic formations of...

This landscape pattern is described in an east-west-north-south (right-left-top-bottom) fashion. How would you rearrange this text to make it easier for people to follow and remember?

Most interactive maps use buttons to light up the locations of places. *Seneca Rocks National Recreation Area, West Virginia.*

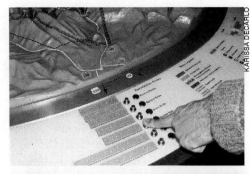

KARISSA DECARLO

Visitors can learn the geography of an area through interactive play. In this exhibit, visitors use their feet to measure the distance traveled by Lewis & Clark. *Missouri River Interpretive Center, Nebraska.*

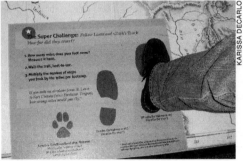

KARISSA DECARLO

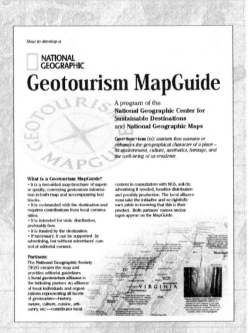

How to develop a

**NATIONAL
GEOGRAPHIC**

Geotourism MapGuide

A program of the
**National Geographic Center for
Sustainable Destinations
and National Geographic Maps**

Geo·tour·ism (n): *tourism that sustains or enhances the geographical character of a place – its environment, culture, aesthetics, heritage, and the well-being of its residents.*

What is a Geotourism MapGuide?
• It is a two-sided map-brochure of superior quality, conveying geotourism information in both map and accompanying text blocks.
• It is co-branded with the destination and requires contributions from local communities.
• It is intended for wide distribution, preferably free.
• It is funded by the destination.
• If necessary, it can be supported by advertising, but without advertisers' control of editorial content.

Partners:
The National Geographic Society (NGS) creates the map and provides editorial guidelines
A local geotourism alliance is the initiating partner. An alliance of local individuals and organizations representing all facets of geotourism—history, nature, culture, cuisine, artisanry, etc.—contributes local content in consultation with NGS, solicits advertising if needed, handles distribution and possibly production. The local alliance must take the initiative and so rightfully earn pride in knowing that this is their product. Both partners' names and/or logos appear on the MapGuide.

Creating a Tourist Map?

If the purpose of your map is to serve as a destination guide for tourists, you may want to take a slightly different approach to planning your map. Check out the National Geographic Geotourism Map Guide at: http://www.nationalgeographic.com/travel/sustainable/pdf/geotourism_mapguide.pdf.

This guide shows you how to create a map of tourist destinations that exemplify the special characteristics of a place. Take a look at page two of the Map Guide for tips on creating "map notes" and "destination dynamics" text blocks.

Step 6: Interaction

Visitors learn about a place either through direct experience with the environment or with a representation of that environment. This experience should involve sensory perception and can be accomplished vicariously by interacting with maps and models. Examples are solid terrain models, fly-through animations, and three-dimensional maps with zooming and panning controls.

Most interactive maps require visitors to push a button that lights up the locations of places. But maps have more potential than this. Interpretive sites can encourage visitors to build a map themselves, pull it apart, take simulated trips over a map, immerse themselves within it, and use it to solve problems.

Interactive play enables visitors to learn the geography of a place and to discover the meaning of a space. Environmental modeling toys and props allow visitors to accomplish spatial tasks, simulate travel, or play games with a spatial component. You will discover techniques for interacting with maps later in this book.

Interview with Tom Patterson, National Park Service Cartographer

Designing interpretive maps is both an art and a science. Perhaps the agency with the most experience in creating interpretive maps is the National Park Service's Harpers Ferry Center. In this section, cartographer Tom Patterson shares his thoughts on the art and science of designing effective maps.

How did you become interested in cartography?
Shaded relief is my major interest in cartography, which began when I was a graduate student at the University of Hawaii in 1980 working on an atlas of American Samoa. One day a mailing tube arrived that influenced the course of my career. Inside was a sheet of drafting film covered with delicate graphite tones—a shaded relief depiction of the complex Samoan landscape. Using only modulated light and shadows, the drawing was easy to understand—and beautiful.

I was inspired to do similar work. After a couple of years of practice, I developed a knack for relief drawing and a style of my own. This arcane craft that I practiced mostly as a hobby eventually landed me a job with National Park Service in 1992, just as digital production was first becoming practical. Now digital techniques allow me to create relief maps in ways that I previously only imagined, mimicking the work of the best cartographic artists. The 391 national park areas are an ideal testing ground for these techniques.

I now work on many more types of maps, including bird's-eye views of historical sites, animations, interactive exhibits, and solid terrain models. The idea of "cartographic realism" guides my approach to map design. When appropriate, and in moderation, I add natural environment effects to a map, effects that people are familiar with and find pleasing—sun glints on water, warm illumination, organic textures, and natural colors.

My goal is to make maps that will attract and hold the attention of readers for as long as possible, encouraging visual exploration. This is what happened to me nearly three decades ago when I saw the shaded relief depiction of Samoa.

What are some of the ways that maps can contribute to the visitor experience?
For the first-time visitor, a map provides a spatial overview of the site. But the role of maps goes well beyond this. They can show information that is not readily apparent—for example, troop movements at a site that today looks more like a manicured park than a battlefield, geologic processes, environmental data, and so on.

Like all successful interpretation, maps can connect the tangible with the intangible allowing the visitor to make a "connection" with the park. Most parks occupy a chunk of geography that lends itself to map depiction. From orientation, to site navigation, to conveying interpretive messages, maps are integral to the visitor experience.

How do you think visitor maps can be improved?
Problematic visitor maps are those that do not focus on the needs of visitors, which is priority number one. One must resist the temptation to fill the limited space on a map with superfluous information, such as administrative matters that are of concern only to those who manage a site.

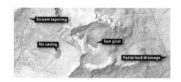

Natural environmental effects contribute to a map's realism. *National Park Service.*

With visitor maps, less is often more. Better still: A map jam-packed with relevant information that doesn't look like it is, which indicates good design. A site visit by the cartographer to meet with park staff and to observe visitors experiencing the park almost always results in better maps.

How does the philosophy for designing interpretive maps differ from conventional cartography?

I think of interpretive maps as a type of thematic map, but aimed at park visitors instead of readers of, say, *National Geographic* magazine or *The Washington Post*. The difference is the audience: Most park visitors are on vacation (and presumably less attentive than when at home), in an unfamiliar environment, and represent a diverse population, including many who lack map-reading experience. Universal design principles are crucially important for such an audience (which potentially includes every person in the world).

What is the most challenging aspect of designing interpretive maps?

Cartographic production is technical. Designing maps is artistic. Developing an interpretive message is pedagogical. Creating successful interpretive maps requires frequent switching between these very different modes of thinking.

Which National Park Service map is your favorite and why?

The map of Eisenhower Farm. For HFC, this map represents a major milestone in digital production and design. In the transition to digital mapping technology over the last dozen years or so, creating bird's-eye views of cultural sites with the detail and artistic flair found in manually produced pieces has been the greatest challenge.

Most computer-generated scenes containing buildings have either synthetic appearance, such as urban scenes in Google Earth, or the brooding ambience found in video games. The Eisenhower map breaks from this tradition. The colors are natural, illumination is warm, textures look real, and the entire scene has a plausibly realistic appearance. The park buildings occupy the highest visual level, helping with legibility.

The Eisenhower map functions as both a device for visitor orientation and as background art that depicts the landscape character. Making the map was painstaking. Everything on it is a three-dimensional wireframe object (draped with textures), including the buildings, trees, fences, and even the grazing cows. It pleases me that the technical underpinnings are completely hidden from view—the map simply looks like an interesting place to visit.

Do you have any final thoughts to share?

Seeing park visitors use the maps that I have made is highly rewarding. Today—for the first time—cartographers have the tools and data available to push the limits of map design with relative ease. Using new technology and data to design better maps for park visitors is, for me, irresistible.

The map of Eisenhower Farm creates a sense of place on paper. *National Park Service.*

Getting Real: Reflecting on the New Look of National Park Service Maps
by Tom Patterson

Excerpted from *Cartographic Perspectives*, Number 43, (Fall, 2002): 43~56. Read the full text at: http://www.shadedrelief.com/realism

The NPS produces tourist maps for 391 parks in a system spanning a large swath of the Earth's surface from the Caribbean to Alaska to the South Pacific, and which is visited by nearly 300 million people each year. Many park visitors are inexperienced map-readers and non-English speakers. In our ongoing effort to make NPS maps accessible to everyone, the design of NPS maps has become less abstract and increasingly realistic.

The move to more realistic map design by the NPS has been gradual and unplanned. Using graphical software applications that allow sophisticated designs to be routinely produced that were previously only imagined, the NPS has found itself inextricably drawn toward using greater realism. The enhanced realism of NPS maps spares the park visitor from the off-putting technical aspects of conventional cartography with maps that are more user-friendly and simultaneously deliver relevant and accurate information.

Webster's dictionary defines realism, in the artistic sense, as: "The picturing in art and literature of people and things as it is thought they really are, without idealizing." Applying this definition to maps is problematic because all maps are idealized representations of the Earth and are inherently abstract.

On the other hand, most of us would agree that some maps appear more realistic and are more intuitively comprehensible than others. For example, a shaded relief map with terrain represented by softly modulated light and shadows appears more realistic than a contour map with a multitude of lines connecting points of equal elevation value. When depicting maps realistically, we are constrained by the finite limits of graphical methods—only so much is possible on a two-dimensional surface—and our pre-conceived ideas of how the Earth appears from above.

With increased realism, map use becomes more a matter of looking rather than reading. By avoiding the use of abstract symbolization, realistic maps have the potential to communicate more efficiently to a greater number of users. Think of this as the cartographic implementation of universal design. Users can comprehend realistically portrayed map information relatively effortlessly without explanation (such as text and legends), so they can spend more of their limited time extracting essential information and examining spatial relationships.

Maps designed in a realistic manner also have the potential to be more attractive, even beautiful, compared to their conventional counterparts. This is not a frivolous concern when trying to connect with audiences. In this media-driven age of short attention spans, it is important that we design maps that attract and hold a reader's attention. People purchase expensive cars based solely on color, vote for telegenic political candidates, and invest substantial sums in corporations that publish slick annual reports. Are map users any less susceptible to the allure of attractive packaging?

With increased realism, maps become more a matter of looking rather than reading. *Canyon de Chelly National Monument, Arizona.*

KARISSA DECARLO

Designing Interpretive Maps

Above: *Chinatown, New York City.*

"Freeman Tilden said that interpretation is an art. A careful artist guides the viewers' eyes to the most important part of the creation. Whatever resource you interpret, always think about what elements you will include and exclude for the benefit of the guest and how you will shape their experience of the resource. It is up to you to frame the visitor's experience so they can look back on it and still recall the mystery and awe of the sometimes hidden and sometimes surprising world we interpret."
—Kirk Carter Mona (*The Interpreter*, September/October 2006)

Maps can lie to your visitors. If a map is not easy to read and understand, people will misinterpret the map's meaning and end up confused, annoyed, or lost.

Designing maps is challenging because there are so many ways to represent information. For instance, multiple graphical variables can be used to symbolize geographic data. These include the size, value, color, shape, texture, arrangement and orientation of point, line, and area symbols. Because maps are complex, interpretive mapmakers should be well versed in cartography.

Cartography involves the art and science of designing maps. Cartographic design can have a huge impact on the way visitors interpret a map. The colors you choose, the placement of text, and the size of graphical symbols can mislead visitors. You can avoid potential problems by familiarizing yourself with the basic principles of cartographic design.

Cartographic Design Principles

This chapter will provide you with map design tips gleaned from the field of cartography. Although you may not be designing maps yourself, it's important for interpretive planners and managers to be involved in the design process. An understanding of the principles of cartographic design will make you a more effective member of the map design team.

Map Title

A map title gives visitors an instant clue to a map's purpose. Titles are generally centered above the map and printed in a larger point size to draw the map-reader's eye. Interpretive maps should have short, thematic titles that reveal the meaning of the space portrayed by the map.

"You Are Here" Symbol

A "You Are Here" symbol is an important feature on visitor maps. This symbol allows visitors to quickly find their position in the landscape and decide which way to go. A "You Are Here" symbol should be printed in a larger type or placed in a call-out box to make it easy to find.

Directional Arrow

A directional arrow is an abbreviated version of a compass rose and indicates which way the map is oriented. Maps

Hazards of rough terrain

If a map is not easy to understand, visitors may end up lost. *Grand Staircase Escalante National Park, Utah.*

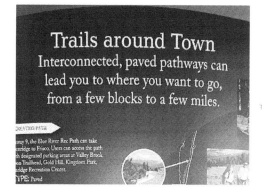
Trails around Town
Interconnected, paved pathways can lead you to where you want to go, from a few blocks to a few miles.

A map title gives visitors an instant clue to a map's purpose. *Breckenridge Welcome Center, Colorado.*

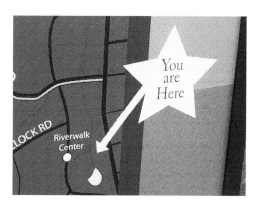
You are Here

A "You Are Here" symbol allows visitors to find their position in the landscape. *Breckenridge Welcome Center, Colorado.*

A directional arrow provides a clue to how a map is oriented. A scale bar offers a clue to how distance on a map compares to distance on the ground. *Red Rock Canyon Open Space, Colorado.*

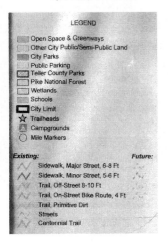

The length of the legend is a measure of the failure of a map.

of larger geographic areas are usually oriented with North at the top, while maps of smaller areas are often oriented to the landscape. Directional arrows are usually placed below the map where they add visual balance to other map elements.

Scale

Use a bar scale to represent distance. That way, if the map is reduced or enlarged, the scale will still be accurate. For hiking and driving maps, you can make them easier to understand by stating the distance between points right on the map. For trails, indicate distances to the tenth of a mile; for driving routes, round to the nearest whole number. If you have a lot of international visitors at your site, it is a good idea to include metric distances as well. If you refer to your map using area units—such as acres—you may want to add a bar scale that helps visitors comprehend area units. (See "How Many Chains is Your Park?" on page 65.)

Labels

Map labels are very much like exhibit labels—the designer must choose a typeface and point size that is easy for visitors to read.

Generally, it's best to stick with a single typeface and use typographic variations to emphasize different elements of the map. This includes varying the point size, text color, and style (like italics or bold). Using two of these variations at once can emphasize differences in labels. For instance, water features are often labeled with *blue italics*.

A minimum type size of 9 or 10 points on printed maps and at least 14 points on signs will make them legible for most visitors. As with exhibits, labels printed in all uppercase letters are difficult to read and should be avoided.

The position of map labels is also an important design consideration. Map symbols should be labeled as follows:

- *Point* labels should be labeled flush left or right either above or below the symbol. Cartographers have identified the order of preference illustrated here.

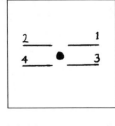

- *Line* labels should try to follow the curve and orientation of line symbols while maintaining legibility.

- *Area* labels should be centered and spread across the area. This can be accomplished on a computer using letter-spacing tools (sometimes called "tracking" or "kerning").

Legends & Symbols

A map legend is like a secret decoder key that tells visitors what a symbol or color on the map means. Most visitors do not have the time or inclination to decode a map. In most cases, if a long legend is needed, the map is probably too complex.

A motto of National Park Service cartographers is, "The length of the legend is a measure of the failure of a map." Simplify maps by using colors and symbols that are self-explanatory. Remember that maps will be read by people who don't share our language, so they should be as easy to understand as possible.

How Many Chains is your Park? Interpreting the Size of Protected Areas

I once read in *Women's Health* magazine that Americans eat 350 slices of pizza per second, which equates to 100 acres of pizza per day. This is an interesting statistic, but I wonder how many people can visualize 100 acres of pizza.

Although the acre continues to be the legal unit of land measurement in the U.S., the United Kingdom (from which the acre was adopted) has converted to the metric system and discourages the use of the acre. Originally the amount of land tillable by a farmer and an ox in one day, this unit of measure has little relevance in modern times. An acre is one furlong (the length of a furrow in a field) in length by one chain in width. Since it was more efficient to plow long narrow strips rather than square plots, an acre was originally thought of as rectangular in shape.

Yet urbanized Americans may be more accustomed to thinking in square feet or miles. Thus, the acre is an unfamiliar unit of measure that continues to be used to report the size of public lands. This results in a vague understanding of the size of large landscapes in the mind of the public. The implication is that people may overestimate the amount of land contained within a protected area or affected by disturbances such as fire or logging. Consider that 16,000 acres may sound like a larger number than 25 square miles, even though they are equal in size.

Few people have knowledge of the relationship between acres and miles (640 acres equals one square mile). When describing the size of areas, managers should relate unfamiliar spatial units to the prior knowledge of visitors. Comparing acres to more common units

Why is it important to preserve this land? MVBSP takes up a few hundred acres—that may seem like a large area, but it's less than a square mile of land. For such a small area, the park contains a large number and variety of plants and wildlife.

of measurement (such as square miles) may help visitors relate the two.

Using analogies such as city blocks or football fields may be useful in visualizing the size of an acre of land. To see how a football field compares to an acre, visit http://en.wikipedia.org/w/index.php?title=Acre&oldid=283402059

Another technique is to design scales that portray area units. For instance, a set of squares can depict 1, 10, 100 and 1000 acres. If you are going to tell visitors that Americans eat 100 acres of pizza a day, make sure they can visualize what this means.

Try this: Encourage visitors to "Adopt an Acre." Have you ever gone to a grocery store and been asked to buy a paper cutout of a shamrock or paw print or some other shape that represents a charity? You write your name on the cutout and they hang it on the wall. You can copy this idea by hanging a large map on your wall. Parcel the map out into individual acres—a small square of paper that represents an acre of space on the map. If visitors donate a dollar, they can write their name on their acre cutout and tape it to the map. This fundraiser has the added benefit of showing your visitors how big one acre of land is compared to the size of the entire area.

The use of acres as a unit of measurement may lead visitors to overestimate the size of protected areas. *Mesilla Valley Bosque State Park, New Mexico.*

Above: Use analogies that compare the size of an area to something familiar. *Alaska Sealife Center.*

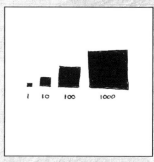

Immediately above: Create a scale bar that portrays units of area such as acres. (This sketch is not to scale.)

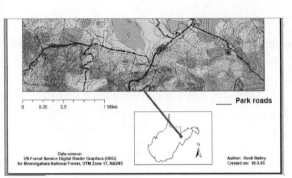

Data source:
US Forest Service Digital Raster Graphics (DRG)
for Monongahela National Forest, UTM Zone 17, NAD83

Park roads

Author: Heidi Bailey
Created on: 10-3-05

The data source
is in the lower left
corner of this map.
The map elements
are arranged to
achieve a balanced,
symmetrical
appearance.

Data Source

Every map should indicate the source of the data used to create the map. This enables users and future designers to determine where and when the data was obtained. Be sure to use current and reliable data sources. Keep in mind that map layers from different sources may have different dates and use different projections. Use place names approved by the Board on Geographic Names (http://geonames.usgs.gov/domestic/).

U.S. government maps are in the public domain and the maps and data may be copied freely. Avoid using maps created by private companies or you may face copyright infringement. You can find free base maps and other data at www.geodata. gov and similar government websites. Most states or universities contain freely accessible GIS layers on the web. You will need GIS software to manipulate the data layers. (Try ArcGIS Explorer—a free downloadable application that offers a simple way to access online GIS content and capabilities—available at www.esri.com/arcgisexplorer.)

To work with shaded relief art, you will need a photo-editing program such as Adobe Photoshop. To draw, color, and position labels, you will need an illustration program like Adobe Illustrator. You can find mapmaking resources such as pre-designed map symbols and techniques for creating shaded relief maps at www.nps.gov/carto.

Balance

Balance refers to the layout of a map's visual components. The elements of a map must be organized in a visually pleasing way much like an exhibit panel or sign. Here are some suggestions for achieving balance:

- The mapped area should be as large as possible. While white space is often used in the layouts of brochures and other media, maps should fill most of the page to make it easier for people to read.

- A map must have symmetry—arrange the various elements so that they balance one another and the map has an overall centered appearance. Spread out map components instead of stacking them on top of each other.

- The title and legend (if one is used) should be more prominent than the north arrow, scale bar, and data source.

- You may need to rearrange map elements a few times to achieve balance. Look for areas that are blank or cramped—is the map top-, bottom-, left-, or right-heavy? Are map elements too close to the edge of the page or are they encroaching on the map itself?

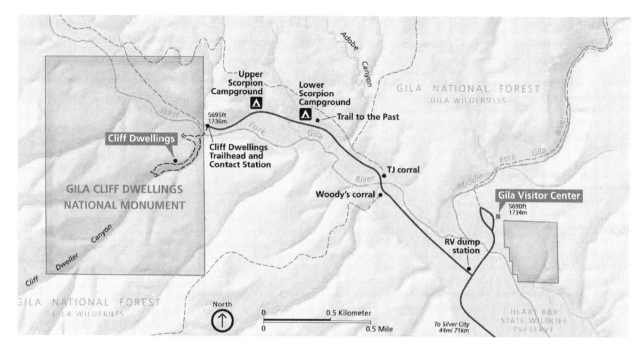

Visual Hierarchy

This is a technique that cartographers use to emphasize certain map features and to make more important places stand out. For example, a map designer will use a larger symbol for the visitor center than for the ranger office. Choosing whether a feature is represented in a strong or subdued manner creates a visual hierarchy that draws a visitor's eyes to the most important places on a map.

Contrast

Contrast is a technique for achieving visual hierarchy. To create visual differences between map features, you can adjust the lightness or darkness of symbols, vary the width of lines, use different type sizes, and choose different shading and patterns. Contrast makes objects pop out against their more subdued backgrounds.

Color

The more abstract a map is, the harder it is for visitors to use. Adding color to a map that mimics the real world can make a map more realistic.

Our eyes are not sensitive to subtle color variations, so use colors that have a strong contrast. For instance, use a light green and a dark green to show the difference between a grassy area and a forest. Shades of green that are too similar will only confuse the eye and the map-reader. Be aware that darker shades attract the eye and lighter shades recede into the background.

This map uses contrast to achieve visual hierarchy. The cliff dwellings and Gila Visitor Center are at the highest visual level. The Gila National Forest and Heart Bar State Wildlife Preserve recede into the background. *Gila Cliff Dwellings National Monument, New Mexico. National Park Service.*

Colors that mimic the real-world landscape give maps a more realistic appearance. *Bryce Canyon National Park, Utah.*

If you will be printing your map in black and white, use only three shades of gray separated by at least 20 percent (i.e. 10 percent, 30 percent, 50 percent). Avoid percentages greater than 50 percent; this will make the shading too dark. If you can afford to print a two-color map, this can make a huge difference in making a map clear. However, don't use the second color merely for decoration.

You should stick to certain cartographic color conventions:

Green—parks, areas of substantial vegetation

White—snow, areas of little or no vegetation

Yellow—deserts, never used for lines or text

Black—grid lines, man-made structures

Red—major roads, safety messages

Brown—contour lines

Blue—water features

Traditional elevation tints can create a false impression of the landscape.

Colors must be chosen carefully or they will invite misinterpretation. For instance, maps with elevation tints are often misunderstood because green is used to represent low-lying areas and browns and golds are used for high areas. This gives the impression of lush vegetation in the lower elevations and barren land in the higher elevations, which may not be true. This color scheme was created by artists over a century ago and has no scientific basis.

Accuracy

Perhaps the most important step in map design is to verify accuracy. Errors in design such as misplaced symbols and labels, distortions in size or relative position, mislabeled or misshaped features, and missing or obsolete data can detract from the effectiveness of visitor maps.

Even accurate maps may be misinterpreted by visitors due to color choices, size of map symbols, and numerous other factors. The important thing is to *review and pretest all visitor maps* and change anything that is inaccurate or produces unintended results.

Part of the design process is to pre-test maps with visitors. *Banff National Park Information Centre, Canada.*

Maps may be enlarged to create signs or wayside exhibits. *Petroglyph National Monument, New Mexico.*

Other Design Considerations

Map Reproduction

Once a map is created, it may be reproduced in many formats, including brochures, signs, exhibits, or downloadable web files. Many potential problems caused by reproduction can be prevented in the design stage:

- Consider how the map will look in black and white. For instance, red on green reproduces poorly in black and white.

- Maps will likely be reduced in size or enlarged to fit different formats. Use a graphic bar scale to ensure that this information remains accurate. A verbal or ratio statement of scale will become inaccurate when resized (one inch will no longer equal one mile on the ground).

- Computer monitors, printers, and projectors can distort map colors. Test any display techniques that you intend to use.

- Web-based maps require special consideration. Too much white on a map can cause eye fatigue when viewed on a monitor. Also, every computer recognizes different fonts. Some map symbols may appear incorrectly on another monitor. One way to prevent this is to save maps as PDF files with embedded fonts.

Top: Maps can be part of an effort to incorporate universal design at an interpretive site. *Kings Mountain National Military Park.*

Immediately above: The prototype of a tactile wayside exhibit panel at Gulf Islands National Seashore.

The map on the right shows how a person with red/green color blindness sees this map of the C&O Canal. *National Park Service.*

Accessibility

"How to convey to a blind man the distances, the heights, the highlights and reflections, and the forests on the crater walls—to say nothing of that blue of the water that has no counterpart?"

—Freeman Tilden

In *The National Parks,* Freeman Tilden tells the story of a blind man who visits Crater Lake and asks an interpreter to describe the park for him. The interpreter takes the man's hands and guides them over a large relief map that depicts the landscape within the park. The blind man feels the size of the lake, the shape of the island, the height of a cliff, the flow of a valley. He recalls a childhood memory of gazing at the blue of the sky. The man sees Crater Lake through his own fingertips and the interpreter's eyes. A map is his window to a new place.

When designing maps and models, it's important to consider the needs of a variety of visitors. Exploring the landscape firsthand may not be possible for some, and accessible maps and models can go a long way in providing spatial context and a sense of place.

Maps can be part of an effort to incorporate universal design at an interpretive site. Low-profile panels are accessible to both visitors with mobility impairments and children. Tactile exhibits and three-dimensional models are accessible to people with sight impairments while providing a tactile experience for all visitors.

Maps and other representations of the landscape can be transformed into tactile exhibits by using raised surfaces to represent landforms, map symbols, and map lines. Various textures can represent land cover, geologic zones, and other spatial patterns. In addition, text can be translated into Braille for blind and low-vision users.

Tactile exhibits can also be created as etched-glass panels; tactile overlays made from molded plastic; acrylic textures embossed onto paper; and signs made by a thermoforming process that uses high heat to mold acrylic panels. Ask your exhibit design firm if they use any of these methods.

In addition to tactile exhibits and low-profile panels, large-print maps can improve accessibility for low-vision users. Maps with large, 18-point type; lines with exaggerated thickness and visual separation; and colors that are readable by people with red/green color blindness are examples of ways that maps can be designed for low-vision users.

More information on accessible maps and exhibits, including a comprehensive white paper on making tactile maps for waysides, is available on the National Park Service website at www.nps.gov/hfc/accessibility.

Coordinating Maps with the Setting
Part of the design process is to find ways of integrating a map with an interpretive setting. Here are some suggestions:

- Match the labels and symbols on signs to the labels and symbols used on visitor maps.

- Use maps to encourage a main route or path through an exhibit area or landscape.

- Emphasize features in the landscape that can serve as landmarks for visitors.

- Use color codes on maps and signs so that visitors instantly know where they are.

- Avoid using numbers on signs and maps unless visitors have to visit places in order.

In Review

The map of Glacier Bay National Park at right illustrates the elements of interpretive map planning and design that we discussed in Chapters 5 and 6:

Theme: The map communicates the theme, "Glaciers Retreat and the Land Rebounds." By showing retreating ice, braided river valleys, and fluctuating coastlines, the map reveals a major characteristic of glacial landscapes: *change.*

Levels: The map of the bay (right side) highlights significant landmarks or points of interest. The series of four smaller maps (upper left) illustrates the route of glacial retreat. The map of the entire park (left center) reveals the overall spatial pattern created by glacial activity in the area.

Type: The map is printed on the largest brochure map size available to the National Park Service. The inset of the bay (right) is oriented to the perspective of the visitor, with the visitor center and entrance to the bay at the bottom of the map.

Visuals: The map uses natural colors (blue, green, white and gray) to create a stylized depiction of the land cover in the park. Shaded relief gives the map a more realistic appearance.

Text: The map contains short blocks of text intended to acquaint visitors with the processes that formed Glacier Bay.

Interaction: Map designers prepared the data in a way that allows the map to be transformed into an interactive computer map, a three-dimensional panorama, fly-through animation, or a solid terrain model.

Cartographic Design: The map designers used larger type sizes, more vivid colors, and graphical embellishments to enhance the visual hierarchy and guide the map-reader's eyes. The effective use of labels and color allowed the designers to simplify the map and forego the use of a legend.

To read more about the design of the Glacier Bay map, visit http://www.nps.gov/hfc/pdf/glba-article.pdf. For more interpretive map examples, browse the National Park Service map gallery on the following pages.

Use the same color codes, labels, and symbols on maps and signs. *Cheyenne Mountain Zoo, Colorado.*

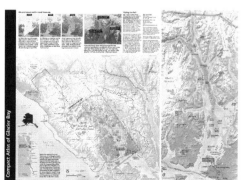

Map brochure of Glacier Bay National Park, Alaska. National Park Service. View a full-size version at: http://www.nps.gov/hfc/pdf/glba-map.pdf.

National Park Service Map Gallery
Courtesy of NPS Harpers Ferry Center

Battlefield—Harpers Ferry National Historical Park, West Virginia
Civil War action of 145 years ago comes to life in this wayside exhibit map that emphasizes the influence of terrain on battlefield strategy. The use of pictorial flags, troops, and cannons rather than conventional military map symbols permits visitors to more easily connect with the past.

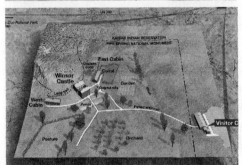

Historic Site—Pipe Spring National Monument, Arizona
Large-scale maps of historical and cultural sites are well suited to three-dimensional depiction—buildings, walkways, and trees appear on the map much as they do to visitors walking the grounds. To establish geographic context, this map shows the small ranch site as an enlarged area set within the wide-open spaces of the Colorado Plateau of northern Arizona. The map was created with 3D software to give it a photo-realistic appearance.

Earth Science—Grand Teton National Park, Wyoming
Jenny Lake fills a basin scooped out by Cascade Canyon Glacier, which melted at the end of the last ice age about 10,000 years ago. By manipulating a Digital Elevation Model (DEM) of the modern landscape in 3D software, we can show what the ancient glacier probably looked like.

Globe—Glacier Bay National Park and Preserve, Alaska
Because most visitors travel great distances to get to remote Glacier Bay, locating the park on a partial globe helps relate it to more familiar places. The foreground shows the Inside Passage route to Glacier Bay from the lower 48 while the background reveals Russia, home to the first Europeans to explore the region. The globe consists of land cover and bathymetry map data draped on a sphere in 3D software.

Interactive Map—Sequoia-Kings Canyon National Park, California
The Zoomify platform creates a high-quality map viewing
experience by allowing users to interact with online map images
using zoom-and-pan controls. View the Sequoia-Kings Canyon
Zoomify map at http://www.nps.gov/hfc/acquisition/maps/
seki-3d.htm.

Panorama—Hawaii Volcanoes National Park, Hawaii
Digitally made in the classical style, panoramas provide sweeping
overviews of park landscapes and feature natural textures and
even clouds. This panorama of Hawaii Volcanoes, created for
an eight-foot-wide display in the visitor center, shows Kilauea
Caldera on the southeast flank of Mauna Loa, the second highest
peak on the big island. View the Hawaii Volcanoes Zoomify map
at http://www.nps.gov/hfc/acquisition/maps/havo-3d.htm.

Map and Panorama—Grand Canyon National Park, Arizona
This panorama shows Grand Canyon Village in the foreground
from a high, map-like angle, and the canyon in the background
from a more oblique angle. The underlying Digital Elevation
Model (DEM) was warped on a cylinder to achieve this effect.
The result is a product that combines the best aspects of a map
and panorama. View the Grand Canyon Zoomify map at http://
www.nps.gov/hfc/acquisition/maps/grca-3d.htm.

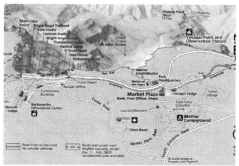

Land Cover—Crater Lake National Park, Oregon
Map colors derive from land cover data that were given forest
canopy and rock textures. This approach yields a hybrid product
with the realism of an aerial photograph and the accuracy and
legibility of a map. The Crater Lake map also shows bathymetry,
allowing visitors to see the hidden world beneath the surface of
the lake.

Trail Map—Mt. Rainier National Park, Washington
With only a quick glance at a three-dimensional trailhead map,
hikers get an understandable image of the terrain that lies ahead
on the trail, including steep sections that might prove difficult.
The recommended orientation of trailhead maps is from a
theoretical point above the trailhead in a bird's-eye view looking
toward the end of the trail. A step-by-step example of trailhead
map design (PowerPoint) is available at http://www.nps.gov/hfc/
acquisition/maps/mora.ppt.

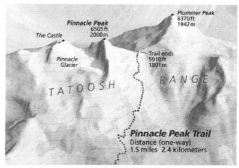

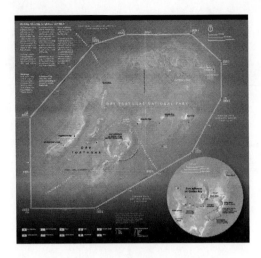

Aerial Photograph—Dry Tortugas National Park, Florida
Rather than map this park in the Gulf of Mexico in a conventional manner with abstract map symbols, the brochure map uses an aerial photograph mosaic for a base. Not only is the aerial photograph beautiful, it clearly shows bottom detail, such as coral, sand, sea grass, and deep water.

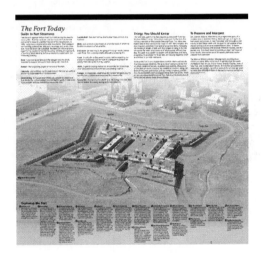

Artistic Illustration—Fort Stanwix National Monument, New York
The bird's-eye view of this fort is based on an oblique aerial photograph shot from a helicopter—the lack of trees around the fort provided a clear view—and manipulated in Photoshop to look like a watercolor painting. The cost was a fraction of what an illustrator would have charged for the project.

Interacting with Maps

"Interpretation's role in exciting people about exploring the landscape is pivotal."

—Joseph Kerski (*Legacy*, May/June 2007)

At the end of Chapter 5, we discovered that visitors learn about a place either through direct experience with an environment or with a representation of that environment. This experience involves sensory perception and can be accomplished by interacting with maps and models.

Most interpretive sites have interactive maps that require visitors to push a button that lights up the locations of places. Sites can improve this interaction by encouraging visitors to create maps themselves, pull maps apart, take simulated trips, and use maps to solve problems.

Maps and environmental modeling toys and props help visitors learn the geography of a place and discover the meaning of a space. The ultimate goal is to excite people about exploring the real-world landscape that a map represents.

Above: *Antelope Canyon, Navajo Parks and Recreation, Arizona.*

Carefully consider the pros and cons of high-tech interactive exhibits.

In this chapter, we will learn how to use maps and related tools to create effective interactive experiences.

Effective Interactive Experiences

Have you noticed that the term *interactive* has become synonymous with *moveable*? Interpretive sites have lots of exhibits with buttons to push, doors that flip, panels that slide, wheels that spin, and electronic screens that change when touched. I took a course in interpretation from a professor who told his students he preferred simple exhibits because interactive exhibits have a tendency to break. He wasn't being quaint; he was being practical.

I travel frequently and I try to stop at every visitor center I come across. I am usually seeking examples of map and geography exhibits, but I also like to observe visitors using exhibits. I have noticed that many people—especially kids—will breeze through an exhibit area pushing, flipping, or spinning anything that is moveable just to see what it does. They don't read it or really look at it—or learn anything from it. They just move on to the next one.

Even worse, visitors can be rough and they will find a way to break things. I recently went to a new heritage center that opened in a town near where I live. The building was beautiful and the exhibits thoughtfully planned, yet several of these carefully designed—and probably expensive—interactive exhibits were broken. This was seven months after the doors had opened and after winter, a time of low visitation. I know every new visitor center needs time to work out the kinks, but I think some of this heartache can be prevented.

For starters, I don't believe an exhibit has to move to be interactive. Since I am usually looking at map exhibits, I have found that push buttons connected to lights embedded in the map are the most common form of map interaction. I find these exhibits to be mindless—they don't engage visitors either emotionally or intellectually.

A key principle of museum learning promoted by the American Association of Museums is that "minds-on" interaction is better than "hands-on" interaction. Instead of asking visitors to push a button that makes a light go on somewhere on the map, try giving them a mental challenge. For example:

What natural landform is in the northwest corner of the map?

Hint 1: Use the compass rose at the bottom of the map to help you find it.

Hint 2: The landform is named after an animal.

Put the answer in small print at the bottom of the panel—no moving parts and your visitors have a chance to make a connection.

If you want an interactive exhibit that is moveable, make the experience value-added. The interaction should relate to the story you are trying to tell. For instance, I used to work at an interpretive site devoted to Lewis and Clark. One of the most popular exhibits was a simulated canoe with a weighted rope attached to it. Visitors pulled the rope and it provided resistance. A scale allowed them to see how far they "moved" the canoe. This exhibit used an interactive element to open visitor's eyes to the challenge Lewis and Clark's team faced when they moved their canoes over land. This was a value-added experience.

A value-added experience with maps should relate to sense of place or map skills (see Chapter 4). Visitors don't need moving parts to interact with maps. Ask them to look at the map, ask them to find something, ask them to think:

Which overlook do you think will provide a better view?

Now go outside and see if you are right!

If you are eager to use some of the high-tech options available today, I have a couple of suggestions. First, put your high-tech map display in its own space and in the hands of your staff. Build an amazing automated or interpreter-led program around the map.

The Colorado History Museum in Denver uses an 8- by 10-foot terrain model, laser projectors, theatrical lights, video monitors,

A question can encourage kids to interact with a map. *Mesilla Valley Bosque State Park, New Mexico.*

Map Questions

What is at...?

Where is...?

What has changed since...?

What pattern do you see...?

What would happen if...?

What do you notice about...?

Imagine traveling through...

Imagine being at a place and looking at...

Can you match the photo of a place to its location on the map?

How are these places similar or different?

How do you think this place came to be?

music, and narration to create a 10-minute program that covers 11,000 years of Colorado history.

I am definitely not saying to eliminate touchable maps. In fact, I think tactile models and environmental modeling toys and props are great spatial learning tools. But keep them low-tech, sturdy, and inexpensive to replace.

Second, invest in an interactive online map. Let visitors use their own high-tech equipment to view it—they will take much better care of their own computers and personal communication devices. You can also set up a computer in your visitor center and encourage people to use the interactive map. If it breaks, remove the monitor while it is being fixed. Keep the screens out of your exhibits so that you don't have unsightly blank screens or holes—that will be what people notice.

Ask a visitor to push a button that turns on a light and the visitor will look at the light. Ask a visitor a question that begs an answer and the visitor will look at the map.

Interacting with Maps

In this section, we will discuss several ways to encourage visitors to interact with maps and the real-world landscape. These techniques involve using flat maps, three-dimensional models, computer-generated maps, living maps, personal communication devices, and navigational tools.

Flat Maps

Convert ordinary flat maps into interactive learning tools by creating "maptivities." Add map activities to the back or around the border of printed maps or add them to map signs and exhibit panels. Here are some maptivity ideas:

Games—Map games can build geography

Maps and models can serve as the centerpiece for interpretive programs. *LumaLore TimeScape map at the Colorado History Museum, Denver.*

Touchable maps and models should be low-tech and sturdy. *Bear Creek Nature Center, Colorado.*

An example of an interactive Maptivity sheet for visitors. *Colorado State Parks.*

and map-reading skills while familiarizing visitors with your site. Create map trivia, map races, or activities that mimic popular board games. Develop find-and-seek games that kids can play in the car or on the trail.

Puzzles—Have you ever looked at the crossword puzzles in airplane magazines? They are frequently filled in by travelers trying to make the time pass. Try adding a crossword puzzle to printed maps. The clues should require the visitor to refer to the map or the actual landscape for answers. You can also make a jigsaw puzzle of your site that visitors must reassemble. Cut out the pieces in a way that requires visitors to connect adjacent point, line, and area features.

Riddles of Place—Add entertaining questions and instructions to printed and exhibit maps: Which scenic overlook would have a better view of the sunset? Plan the shortest possible route through the park that will take you by each of these places. How can you get from Point A to Point B without taking any left turns? Where would you be if you ate lunch at a picnic area along the banks of the _____ River?

Map Skills—Visitors can sharpen their map-reading skills by using scale bars, legends, grids, contours, map symbols, and other map elements to discover interesting facts about your site. Instead of telling visitors what the highest place in the park is—encourage them to find out for themselves.

Spatial Thinking—This skill involves mental rotation, remembering routes, understanding scale, and three-dimensional visualization. Ask visitors to match the top view of a building or landform with its side view; test their ability to remember a route or the layout of an area, group items according to scale, or remember the appearance of a landmark after viewing a photo (size, shape, color, etc).

Three-Dimensional Maps & Models

Anaglyphs
Anaglyph photos and maps are created by printing two slightly offset (stereoscopic) images on top of each other. Two color layers are used to create the effect—a red image is pasted on top of a cyan image. When the viewer dons a pair of three-dimensional glasses, the image appears three-dimensional. Anaglyph maps offer an alternative to topographic models when space or funding is an issue. Learn to create anaglyph images: http://3dparks. wr.usgs.gov/3Dbayarea/html/aboutthissite.htm

KID TIP: Let the kids hold the map and follow along as you drive.

Encourage kids to use a map in the car or on the trail. *Pikes Peak Heritage Center, Colorado.*

Anaglyph maps appear three-dimensional when the viewer wears a pair of three-dimensional glasses. *Mesilla Valley Bosque State Park, New Mexico.*

A solid terrain model placed near an entranceway can draw visitors into an exhibit area. *Mesilla Valley Bosque State Park, New Mexico.*

Interpreters and visitors can use solid terrain models to point out landscape features and spatial relationships. *North Rim Visitor Center, Grand Canyon National Park, Arizona.*

Solid Terrain Models

A solid terrain model is a physical model that visitors can gather around, view from all directions, and sometimes explore with their hands. These models are usually several square feet in size and are displayed on tabletops or walls. A spectacular solid terrain model strategically placed near a window or entranceway can draw visitors into a building or exhibit area. These models can often be created from the same data and imagery that is used to make printed maps. To see how they are made, visit http://www.nps.gov/hfc/acquisition/map-contracts-1.htm.

Interpreters can transform static models into interactive exhibits by using pointing devices. When communicating information about a landscape, pointing focuses attention on places, paths, and patterns. Pointing is a technique that can easily be incorporated into interpretive programs by allowing visitors to locate and point out features and their spatial relationships. Solid terrain models can be animated with lasers, projectors, fiber optics, or even a light pen.

Interpreters at Grand Teton National Park use the solid terrain model at the Craig Thomas Discovery Center for their "Map Chat," a 30-minute talk about wildlife. The interpreters point out landscape patterns on the map that can help visitors find and view wildlife in their natural habitats. Colors on the map represent different types of vegetation and are directly related to the types of wildlife that can be found in these areas.

Solid terrain models' life-like appearance makes them ideally suited to interpreting stories about places, paths, and patterns. See the world's largest example at: http://www.stm-usa.com/bc.htm.

Computerized Maps and Models

These maps are delivered on the Internet or other types of electronic devices. The programs typically offer user interfaces that allow visitors to manipulate map elements. The most basic computerized maps are high-resolution digital versions of park maps that allow visitors to zoom and pan to focus on specific map features. More sophisticated computerized maps include animated maps, virtual models, and Geographic Information Systems.

Animated Maps

Animated maps come in two forms—fly-through animations and motion simulations. Fly-through animations take visitors on a virtual journey over a simulated landscape. These maps are created from digital elevation data and satellite imagery. Motion simulations depict thematic information—such as the movement of glaciers—with virtual movement. To see examples of both types of animated maps, visit http://www.nps.gov/hfc/acquisition/map-contracts-3.htm.

You can download the article, *Tips for Designing Effective Animated Maps*, by Mark Harrower at: http://www.geography.wisc.edu/~harrower/pdf/CP_Harrower2004.pdf.

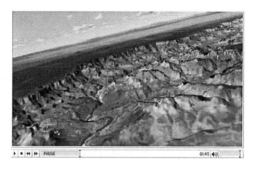

Follow this link to view a fly-through animation of Grand Canyon National Park, Arizona: http://www.nps.gov/grca/photosmultimedia/fly-through.htm.

Virtual Models

Internet-based mapping programs allow users to travel through virtual space, zoom to different scales, and rotate the landscape to allow different perspectives. Google Earth and NASA World Wind are both satellite image-based mapping programs available for free download. These three-dimensional virtual worlds make excellent visual aids as they can be projected onto a screen or wall.

These programs offer users the unprecedented ability of being able to travel through a landscape in virtual space. A computer with Internet capability at a visitor center can enable visitors to explore the area from a variety of different directions and vantage points. Google Earth and similar systems allow users to rotate the landscape to achieve a birds-eye or oblique view of an area while moving between places and traveling simulated routes.

These programs are powerful tools for learning the configuration of a landscape; however, there are certain issues that must be addressed. First, the resolution of the imagery depicting natural areas is often not as high as the resolution of urban areas. Thus, not all sites will be represented adequately. Second, adjacent satellite images may have been taken on different dates, in different seasons, or at different resolutions. These issues can degrade the quality of the three-dimensional

Virtual model of Mount St. Helen's. *NASA World Wind Screen Shot.*

view of a place. Finally, content added by other users can be incorrectly placed and may contain erroneous information.

Despite these concerns, three-dimensional virtual worlds offer a powerful interpretive opportunity by enabling visitors to visualize new landscapes. Visit http://earth.google.com/outreach/index.html for information on using Google Earth to create maps and virtual trips to your site.

Geographic Information Systems (GIS)

Though it sounds complex, the basic concept of GIS is quite simple. Bits and pieces of maps and data are stored in a computer as separate files and databases. These pieces can be put together to make something new. Think of your favorite recipe—all of the ingredients are stored separately until you take them out of your cabinet and mix them together to make a meal. A GIS is a computer program that allows you to mix different data and map pieces together to create a customized map.

A GIS is kind of like your computer desktop. You can add a background photo of your cat to your desktop, choose the icons you want to appear, and add labels so you know what each icon means. In a GIS, you can add a background image of an air photo, satellite image, or topographic map. Then you can add icons, or symbols, that show towns, roads, or other map pieces. These symbols are georeferenced, which means they will show up in the right location on your map. The computer remembers this information just like it remembers where to place the icons on your desktop each time you turn on your computer. Finally, you can add a layer that shows the names of each of the places on your map.

If you haven't worked with computers much, think of the transparency sheets that teachers sometimes use with overhead projectors. Each transparency can have different information or parts of a picture that make a complete image when they are stacked on top of each other. Different transparency layers can be added or removed as needed.

GIS allows people to manipulate multiple layers of information. This is a great way to create an exhibit that focuses on the three Ps—places, paths, and patterns. Visitors can turn these layers, or levels of information, on and off to break the map into easily digestible "chunks." These layers can be displayed on a computer screen or projected onto a three-dimensional model.

The real power of a GIS is for problem solving. A GIS allows users to take data from a table and display this information on a map. This enables planners and managers to see landscape patterns and make decisions. For example, a map created in a GIS can show the best place to build a visitor center based on the locations of flood zones, viewsheds, and habitat areas.

GIS layers can be projected onto a three-dimensional model. *www.360parks.com.*

Living Maps

Living maps are maps painted on large canvases that can be rolled up, transported, and used in a variety of settings. Program participants use various props to bring the map to life. Living maps facilitate discussions about spatial relationships pertaining to subjects ranging from history and culture to geology and ecology.

The power of living maps is that they allow visitors to build a map themselves and then to explore and travel within the map. By allowing visitors to become part of the map, the space it represents can come to life.

The following instructions for creating a living map were taken from two articles written by Gary Bremen of the National Park Service: "The Living Map" (*Legacy*, 1992) and "The Living Map: Bridging the Gap" (*National Interpreters Workshop Proceedings*, 1992).

How to Create a Living Map

1. Measure and draw a grid of small squares on a map of your interpretive site. The number and size of these squares will be determined by the size of the map and by how detailed it is. One-inch squares are an easy figure to work with.

2. Decide on a size for the finished map. This may be determined by the size of your presentation area, the size of your vehicle (if you will be taking the map off-site), or the cost of the canvas. A canvas weight of #12 artist's duck works well. Seams have little effect on the finished product and may save you money.

3. Measure and mark the location of each grid line on the *edge* of the canvas using permanent markers. Use the same proportion that you used on your small map (for example, one inch equals one foot). Don't draw grid lines across the canvas, as they may bleed through on the finished product.

4. Apply a base coat of high-quality gesso to the entire canvas. Thin the gesso with water until it is the consistency of pancake batter. If one color is predominant on your map, tint the gesso this color with acrylic paint. The gesso can be applied with long-handled rollers, but be careful not to apply it too thickly or it might crack. The base coat accomplishes several things: it adds strength, ensures even shrinkage of the canvas, and provides a surface on which to apply other colors later.

5. Sketch the map details with a soft lead pencil. To begin, stretch lengths of yarn across the map and tape them at the marks you made earlier on the edges of the canvas. The yarn will

Top: A living map is painted on a large canvas that can be used in a variety of settings. *Nauticus, Virginia.*

COURTESY OF GARY BREMEN

Living maps allow visitors to become part of a map. *Biscayne National Park.*

form a moveable grid with squares that are proportional to the squares on your small map. Now draw in the details one square at a time. Include only natural physical features—your visitors will add buildings, roads and place names later.

6. When the drawing is complete, bring the map to life with color. Acrylics, which are fast drying and easy to clean up, should be used for the entire project. Paint prices vary tremendously with color—be sure to choose your colors carefully. Mixing your own shades from a few basic colors will save money. Large areas can be painted with rollers and large house-painting brushes, while details can be done with small artist's brushes. This part of the process is probably the most enjoyable, since many people can participate together.

7. Finally, gather props for the map. Natural objects from the interpretive site, reproduction artifacts, herbarium samples, magazine pictures, study skins, and toys from rummage sales are just a few possibilities. Place names can be printed on brightly colored paper and laminated for durability. A brainstorming session can yield scores of ideas.

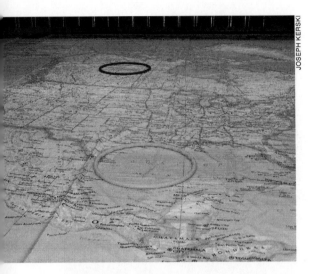

National Geographic rents living maps for use in geography education (http://ngsednet.org/ community/about.cfm?community_id=515).

How to Use a Living Map
Invite participants to take off their shoes and sit around the edges of the map. One way to introduce the map is to hand people a place name card when they arrive and ask them to place it in the appropriate location. Encourage other participants to help.

Depending on the theme of your program, have participants continue to build the map using various props (photos, blocks, toys, shells, pinecones, yarn for paths/boundaries, etc). Lead a discussion that focuses on the importance of places, paths, and spatial patterns.

The potential uses of a living map are limited only by the imagination of the interpreter presenting the program. A living map's interdisciplinary nature allows it to fit in with virtually any curriculum. A living map can go a long way in bridging gaps in a visitor's understanding of an interpretive site.

The Mapped World

There is nothing like the real thing. Encourage people to use maps to explore the environment firsthand. In this section, we will look at several ways to encourage visitors to interact with maps and the real-world environments they represent.

Linking Maps to Cell Phone Tours and Podcasts

Cell phone tours and podcasts offer an alternative for reaching visitors who do not attend programs or browse exhibits. Many visitors are seeking a snippet of information where they are physically located at the time. Cell phone tours and podcasts allow visitors to use their own devices to access interpretive content wherever and whenever they want.

A cell phone tour is composed of a series of prerecorded messages that visitors can access by dialing a unique phone number. Items on the tour are identified by symbols placed on signs or printed on a map brochure. When visitors find an item of interest, they can enter a short numerical code to access the desired message. There is no cost to the visitor other than the minutes charged by their phone service.

Podcasts are downloadable audio programs that replace the old radio or headset style of self-guided audio tours. Visitors can download these files to a portable mp3 player and listen to them as they travel through an interpretive site. Some places offer video podcasts in addition to the audio programs.

These technologies allow managers to track what messages people listen to and how long they listen. This enables interpretive sites to continuously improve and update content. For instance, while most programs run two minutes, NPS sites have discovered that most users only listen for about 90 seconds, and have shortened their programs accordingly. For more information about cell phone tours and podcasts, visit www.parkcast.com and www.guidebycell.com.

Some interpretive sites offer similar devices that visitors can check out or rent. Often called "GPS rangers," these personal data devices are automatically triggered when a visitor passes near a certain geographic coordinate. A short interpretive program is delivered on the spot using a mix of audio, video, text, and sound effects.

In the future, interpretive sites may become "clickable." A technology is available that allows anyone to create digital tags or barcodes online, print them out, and post them in real-world places. Visitors with the appropriate software loaded on their cell phones can decode the digital tag, which connects them to a web

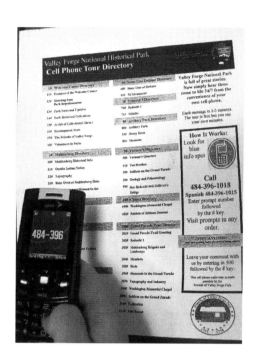

Cell phone tours enable visitors to access interpretive content whenever and wherever they want. *Valley Forge National Historic Park, Pennsylvania.*

page. These real-world hyperlinks offer a way to connect the virtual and physical worlds. For information, visit http://www.tag.cx/ and www.semapedia.org.

For more information on creating cell phone tours and podcasts, see Appendix 1.

Global Positioning Systems (GPS)
GPS is an acronym for Global Positioning System. It means exactly what the term implies: a system for precisely determining your position anywhere on the globe. This is made possible by a network of satellites that continuously transmits coded information. A handheld GPS receiver figures out a user's coordinates based on this data.

A GPS receiver calculates your location in much the same way that you can figure out a storm's distance by counting the number of seconds between a lightning flash and thunder. A GPS receiver multiplies the velocity of the transmitted signal by the time it takes the signal to reach you—the longer it takes, the farther away it is.

A GPS receiver needs to talk to at least four satellites in order to determine your three-dimensional position (latitude, longitude, and altitude). GPS satellites transmit extremely low-power signals of about 20–50 watts. Compare this to an FM radio station that transmits at 100,000 watts. While your favorite radio station may be located in the next town, GPS satellites are 12,000 miles away.

For this reason, you may have difficulty picking up satellites in thick foliage, close to high buildings, or near steep terrain. GPS units will generally not work indoors, underwater, or underground. Although GPS is an amazing technology, it does have limitations, thus GPS users should also know how to navigate using a map and compass.

GPS receivers are becoming increasingly popular as both recreation and management tools. Receivers can be found in cars, cell phones, handheld units, and wristwatches. Newer GPS receivers allow you to load topographic and road maps, satellite photography, and even real-time weather data.

As you travel, your GPS receiver will record your progress in a track log. GPS tracks are often referred to as "bread crumb trails" that show exactly where you've been. You can use this information to record routes and even generate a vertical profile of the terrain. Some ski areas rent out armband GPS units that track a people's skiing and snowboarding excursions. At the end of the day, visitors leave with a personalized ski area map as a souvenir.

A GPS receiver also allows users to record and enter waypoints. A waypoint is a set of coordinates for a specific place, such as a trailhead or scenic overlook. A GPS receiver can guide you to a waypoint while keeping track of where you are, how far you are from your destination, how fast you are traveling, and when you will arrive.

Interpretive sites can provide waypoint information to visitors in addition to traditional trail maps. Waypoints can be collected by staff and volunteers that are trained to use GPS receivers. Many trails have already been mapped by GPS fans, and you can search to see if the waypointing work for your site has already been done. Start your search at http://travelbygps.com/search.php and http://www.wikiloc.com/wikiloc/home.do. Double-check all waypoints for accuracy.

Borrow this idea from *Backpacker* magazine: Create pocket-size maps with waypoints for hiking trails, walking tours, and other routes.

Top: A handheld GPS receiver.

Immediately above: These pocket-size trail maps from Backpacker magazine provide visitors with GPS waypoints.

GPS Activities

Geocaching—This activity is a high-tech version of a scavenger hunt in which participants use a GPS receiver to find a secret stash hidden in the landscape. Participants log on to a geocaching website to obtain the coordinates of the secret stash, or "cache." The cache is usually a plastic container that contains a logbook and a small treasure. Finders can take the treasure as a souvenir as long as they leave a new trinket for the next finder. To learn more, see "Using Geocaches to Spread Interpretive Messages to New Audiences" at http://www.interpnet.com/download/geocache.pdf.

Waymarking—Waymarks are sometimes called "virtual" caches. The location itself is the treasure, and no physical object is placed at the spot. This sport allows fans of geocaching to enjoy locations that are off-limits to traditional caches. Participants record their visit in an online logbook that may require them to answer questions or upload a photo to prove they were there. For more information, visit http://www.earthcache.org.

Benchmarking—Also known as survey mark hunting, this activity takes people in search of small metal disks that physically mark the location of geographic coordinates. In the U.S., geographic reference points are maintained by NOAA's National Geodetic Survey. Visit www.

HEIDI BAILEY

Geocachers seek a secret stash hidden within the landscape.

Benchmarks show the physical locations of geographic reference points. *Nauticus, Virginia*.

geocaching.com/mark.

Confluence Hunting—In this activity, GPS enthusiasts visit sites where integer lines of latitude and longitude converge. There's a confluence point within 50 miles of where you are right now. To find it, visit www.confluence.org to obtain coordinates, photos, and trip reports.

Letterboxing—This activity is similar to geocaching, but GPS is not required. Letterboxing works in much the same way as a traditional scavenger hunt, with participants following clues to find a hidden treasure. This activity is popular with children and families. Letterboxers carry a journal, personal stamp, and an inkpad. When a cache is discovered, finders leave an imprint of their personal stamps in the cache logbook, and then stamp their personal journal with the stamp stored in the cache. Visit www.letterboxing.org for more information.

Orienteering—This is a competitive sport that requires participants to use a map and compass to find a series of hidden flags. Competitors race against each other to be the first person to discover all of the flags in order. Learn more at http://www.us.orienteering.org/.

Avoid Geo-Trashing. Sites should be familiar with the potential impacts of geocaching activities. Visit http://www.geocachingpolicy.info/ to read sample management policies regarding geocaching.

A letterboxing kit: journal, rubber stamp, and inkpad.

An orienteering map and compass. *Florissant Fossil Beds National Monument, Colorado.*

"It is in parks and museums where many people first start to realize the fragile state of Earth affairs and start appreciating a landscape in the true sense of the word. The connection between interpretation and geography is not just a nice thing or a useful thing—it is a critical thing, critical not only for that local site, but for the planet."

—Dr. Joseph Kerski, ESRI

Putting Interpretation on the Map

Do you remember the girl from Chapter 1—the one with more than 200 Junior Ranger badges? Here is the rest of her story:

The letter the girl wrote to the volunteers and staff of Florissant Fossil Beds National Monument passed from person to person until everyone knew her story. At the time, one of the volunteers—a woman named Sally—was in the midst of planning an important event. She and members of 14 educational organizations and interpretive sites were coordinating Colorado's first No Child Left Inside Weekend.

Sally had arranged for the weekend of outdoor-oriented

Above: *Everglades National Park, Florida.*

Heidi Bailey **89**

activities to be kicked off by a talk from *Last Child in the Woods* author Richard Louv. When Sally read the young girl's letter, she made a sudden decision—she would invite the enthusiastic Junior Ranger to introduce Louv to the more than 2,000 people attending the opening ceremonies.

Sally made arrangements for the girl to fly to Colorado from her home in Georgia. During her stay, the girl participated in the No Child Left Inside Weekend activities and inducted over 125 new members into the Junior Ranger program.

On the night of Louv's speech, the girl stood before an entire auditorium of people to deliver the opening remarks for the world-famous author's presentation. But before she turned the stage over to Louv, she gave a little presentation of her own.

The girl brought forth a piece of paper, a certificate proclaiming her admission into the Junior Ranger program. The document was signed and dated by the volunteer at Florissant Fossil Beds National Monument who had introduced her to the program over six years before.

That volunteer was Sally.

Everyday at sites around the world, interpreters like Sally forge bonds between people and places. Interpreters who understand the principles of geography are also able to connect people to the bigger picture: an image of our planet as a place of complex relationships and intricate spatial patterns.

Although we are born with an innate ability to think spatially, this is a skill that must be cultivated beginning in early childhood and continuing throughout our adult lives. "Childhood is a branch of cartography," says Michael Chabon in *Children's Lost Wilderness* (http://www.nybooks.com/articles/22891). Chabon refers to the way children physically explore and mentally map their worlds.

We can take this idea a step further and say that adulthood is a branch of geography. As we mature, we grow into people who are capable of understanding the complex relationships between the natural and cultural worlds. We can develop into spatial thinkers who seek out patterns in the landscape and use this information to make responsible choices.

These decisions may be as simple as choosing where we want to live or as complex as determining how to vote on a land use proposal. In the end, geographic knowledge does not have to do with knowing where places are, but with our ability to act as skilled spatial thinkers.

This book has been an attempt at putting the tools of geography in your hands. I encourage you to use these tools to communicate the interconnectedness of places on the Earth with the goal of improving people's spatial knowledge and decision-making abilities.

Some day, geographers hope that courses in spatial literacy will become an integral part of the curriculum in schools and universities. But until that day comes, interpreters can contribute to this goal by helping people connect with places, visualize landscape patterns, understand communities, and use maps to explore the environment.

Always remember that interpreters are geographers. And never forget that what you do is important not only for your site, but for the world.

Sally and Chandler

Bibliography

Arthur, P., & Passini, R. (1992). *Wayfinding: People, Signs, and Architecture.* New York: McGraw-Hill Book Company.

Bailey, H., Smaldone, B., Elmes, G. & Burns, R. (2007). Geointerpretation: The interpretive potential of maps. *Journal of Interpretation Research, 12*(2), 45-59.

Bell, N. (1982). *The Book of Where: How to Be Naturally Geographic.* New York: Scholastic.

Bremen, G. (1992 July/August). The Living Map. *Legacy 3*(4), 10-14.

Bremen, G., Albrecht, B., Dale, M., & Hertel, E. (1992). The living map: Bridging the gap. *1992 National Interpreters Workshop Proceedings*, 216-219.

Brochu, L. & Merriman, T. (2002). *Personal Interpretation: Connecting Your Audience to Heritage Resources.* Fort Collins, CO: InterpPress.

Clebsch, J.C., & Curwen, J. (2000). GIS-Geographic Information Systems and Good Interpretive Services. *2000 Interpretive Sourcebook*, 207-209.

Cohen, M.S., Winkel, G.H., Olsen, R., & Wheeler, F. (1977). Orientation in a museum: An experimental visitor study. *Curator, 20*(2), 85-107.

Cornell, J. (1998). *Sharing Nature with Children*, 2nd ed. Nevada City, CA: Dawn Publications.

Cresswell, T. (2004). *Place: A Short Introduction.* Malden, MA: Blackwell Publishing.

Davis, K.C. (1992). *Don't Know Much About Geography.* New York: William Morrow and Company.

Dent, B. (1972). Visual organization and thematic map communication. *Annals of the Association of American Geographers, 62*(1), 79-93.

Dill, Bonnie (1994). *Teaching the Five Themes of Geography.* Frank Schaffer Publications: Torrance, California.

Dobson, J.E. (2007 Spring). Bring back geography! *ArcNews, 29*(1), 1-5.

Downs, R., & Stea, D. (1977). *Maps in Minds: Reflections on Cognitive Mapping.* New York: Harper and Row.

Dransch D. (2000). The use of different media in visualizing spatial data, *Computers & Geosciences, 26*(1), 5-9.

Evans, C., Butcher, G., Dufficy, T., & Hamel, C. (1999). From a bird's-eye view to satellite images—changing views of your park. *1999 Interpretive Sourcebook*, 73-76.

Freundschuh, S.M., & Egenhofer, M.J. (1997). Human conceptions of spaces: implications for GIS. *Transactions in GIS, 2*(4), 361-375.

Garmin (2000). *GPS Guide for Beginners.* Olathe, KS: Garmin International, Inc.

Golledge, R.G. (1992). Place recognition and wayfinding: Making sense of space. *Geoforum, 23*(2), 199-214.

Golledge, R.G., & Stimson, R.J. (1997). *Spatial Behavior: A Geographic Perspective.* New York: Guilford Press.

Gross, M., & Zimmerman, R. (2002). *Interpretive centers: The history, design and development of nature and visitor centers.* Stevens Point, WI: UW-SP Foundation Press, Inc.

Guy, B.S., Curtis, W.W., & Crotts, J.C. (1990). Environmental learning of first-time travelers. *Annals of Tourism Research, 17,* 419-431.

Hall, C.M., & Page, S.J. (2002). *The Geography of Tourism and Recreation: Environment, Place and Space,* 2nd ed. London & New York: Routledge.

Ham, S.H. (1992). *Environmental Interpretation: A Practical Guide for People with Big Ideas and Small Budgets.* Golden, CO: Fulcrum Publishing.

Kealy, M. (1998). *Mapmaking for parklands. Information Design: Tools and Techniques for Park Produced Publications.* National Park Service: U.S. Dept. of the Interior, p 31-51.

Kealy, M. (1998). Lost? Don't blame the map: Designing maps for visitors. *1998 Interpretive Sourcebook,* 172-174.

Kelley, V.C. (1982). *Albuquerque: Its Mountains, Valley, Water, and Volcanoes.* Socorro, N.M.: Bureau of Mines & Mineral Resources.

Kerski, J.J. (2007 May/June). What's really important in interpreting climate change. *Legacy,* p 34-37.

Kerski, J.J., & Reiter, S. (2004). Interpreting the landscape with USGS maps, aerial photographs and GPS. *2004 Interpretive Sourcebook,* 138-139.

Kitchin, R.M. (1997). Exploring spatial thought. *Environment and Behavior, 29*(1), 123-156.

Knopf, R.C. (1981). Cognitive map formation as a tool for facilitating information transfer in interpretive programming. *Journal of Leisure Research, 13*(3), 232-242.

Levine, M., Marchon, I., & Hanley, G. (1984). The placement and misplacement of you-are-here maps. *Environment and Behavior 16*(2), 139-157.

Lewis, W.J. (1989). *Interpreting for Park Visitors.* Philadelphia, PA: Eastern Acorn Press.

Littlejohn, M.A., Meldrum, B.H., & Hollenhorst, S.J. (2006). *Yosemite National Park Visitor Study, NPS VSP Report 168,* 103 p.

Louv, R. (2005). *Last Child in the Woods.* Chapel Hill, NC: Algonquin Books.

Mandl, H., & Levin, J.R. (1989). *Knowledge Acquisition from Text and Pictures.* Amsterdam: Elsevier.

McKendry, J.E. (2000). The influence of map design on resource management decision making. *Cartographica, 37*(2), 13-25.

Medyckyj-Scott, D., & Blades, M. (1992). Human spatial cognition: Its relevance to the design and use of spatial information systems. *Geoforum, 23*(2), 215-226.

Monmonier, M. (1993). *Mapping it Out.* Chicago: University of Chicago Press.

Monmonier, M. (1991). *How to Lie with Maps.* Chicago: University of Chicago Press.

Moscardo, G. (1999). *Making Visitors Mindful: Principles for Creating Sustainable Visitor Experiences through Effective Communication*. Champaign, IL: Sagamore.

National Geographic. The Five Themes of Geography. Retrieved June 2008 from http://www.nationalgeographic.com/resources/ngo/education/themes.html.

National Park Service (2007 Nov/Dec). *HFC onMedia: Issue on Accessibility for NPS Interpretive Media*. U.S. Dept. of the Interior: Harpers Ferry Center Media Services.

National Park Service (2005). *Map Standards*. U.S. Dept. of the Interior: Harpers Ferry Center Media Services.

National Research Council (2006). *Learning to Think Spatially*. Washington, D.C.: National Academies Press.

Patterson, T. (2002). Getting real: Reflecting on the new look of National Park Service maps. *Proceedings of International Cartographic Association (ICA) Mountain Cartography Workshop*. Mt. Hood, OR.

Patterson, T. (n.d.). Developing a new visitor map of Glacier Bay National Park, Alaska. Retrieved October 2006 from http://www.nps.gov/hfc/pdf/glba-article.pdf.

Pearce, P.L., & Black, N. (1984). Dimensions of national park maps: A psychological evaluation. *Cartography, 13*(3), 189-203.

Peuquet, D.J. (2002). *Representations of Space and Time*. New York: Guilford Press.

Redvale, J., & Dickey, E. (1995). Hands-on exhibits: The magical touch. *The 1995 Interpretive Sourcebook*, 199-201.

Schobesberger, D. (2007). Evaluating the effectiveness of 2D vs. 3D trailhead maps. Retrieved October 2007 from http://www.nps.gov/hfc/carto/zion_map_study.pdf.

Sexton, P. (2008). Interpretation using Google Earth. *NAI National Workshop Interpretive Sourcebook*, 146-147.

Sobel, D. (1998). *Mapmaking With Children: Sense of Place Education for the Elementary Years*. Portsmouth, N.H.: Heinemann.

Talbot, J.F., Kaplan, R., Kuo, F.E., & Kaplan, S. (1993). Factors that enhance effectiveness of visitor maps. *Environment and Behavior, 25*(6), 743-760.

Thorndyke, P.W., & Stasz, C. (1980). Individual differences in procedures for knowledge acquisition from maps. *Cognitive Psychology, 12*, 137-175.

Tilden, F. (1957). *Interpreting Our Heritage*. Chapel Hill: University of North Carolina Press.

Turnbull, D. (1989). *Maps are Territories*. Chicago: University of Chicago Press.

Vander Stoep, G.A. (1990). Aerial photos and other views from above: New ways to tell old stories. *1990 National Interpreters Workshop Proceedings*, 92-94.

Warren, D.H., & Scott, T.E. (1993). Map alignment in traveling multisegment routes. *Environment and Behavior, 25*(5), 643-666.

Young, M. (1999). Cognitive maps of nature-based tourists. *Annals of Tourism Research, 26*(4), 817-839.

Appendix

How to Build Your Own Podcasts and Cell Phone Tours

Script Development

- Imagine you are standing at the location with the visitor and speaking directly to him/her.

- Be excited to be at the location.

- Keep sentences short. Use two or three sentences instead of one long one.

- Be conversational—never appear to be "lecturing" the visitor. No one wants a companion who is a "know it all" even if you are a guide.

- Use the question technique, "How many different layers of rock can you identify in the colorful walls of the Grand Canyon?" The visitor will begin searching the canyon and trying to count layers (interactive).

- Combine facts and substance about historic locations with a lighter story. Perhaps something humorous took place there or something chilling like murder or death!

- When you present facts, always phrase them as "historians have discovered" or "we've come to believe." That puts you more as a discoverer rather than a lecturer.

- Use vivid adjectives and action verbs. Waterfalls "cascade" rather than spill over. Military statues "guard" or "patrol" the square rather than just standing there. Lights shimmer rather than burn, illuminate rather than light.

- Recognize that you are on a visit together. If you have to move somewhere, say "from here we can see another exciting exhibit, just 50 yards west."

- Put the visitor in the company of other visitors. "Many visitors to this location have asked about . . . " Your visitor might just have the same question in mind and answering it for him or her will make you seem more like a companion.

- Don't be afraid to give facts—visitors like facts—but never give too many at once. One good fact that illuminates the experience is better than three piled on together.

- Read your final script out loud to "hear and feel" how it sounds.

Audio and Video Components

- A written script is recommended for most presenters. It insures that all desired content is captured during filming and makes the video editing easier.

- Videos should run no longer than two minutes to maintain viewer attention.

- Audio only tour segments should be limited to 90 seconds.

- Hand-held devices offer a small screen. Images and video should be close up to give more detail.

- Film your host in front of a darker background.

- Use a tripod to avoid camera movement.

- When shooting outside, use a reflector to highlight the face (essential when shooting a host with a hat).

- Try putting the host in full sunlight with the sun behind the camera instead of in the shade. In the shade, make sure the light is even on the face.

- When shooting indoors, a lighting kit should be used.

- Use a lapel microphone and/or a boom mike to capture clear audio.

- Capture two or three takes of the same segment for fall back.

- If time permits (and you have a written script) have the host record the entire audio off camera. The voice over audio can be used for cut away to stills or other footage.

- Select music and sound effects to compliment the tour. Online sources are sold with rights.

- Export video using a high quality "same as source" format such as a .mov.

- For audio only tours invest in a hand-held digital recorder and microphone.

- Digital MP3 files can be uploaded directly to cell phone systems.

Images

- Selecting the right images is essential to a great tour. Gather images to follow the script. One image per thought is recommended. Generally, one sentence is one complete thought.

- When the script refers to a specific item or list of items, display an image of each one.

- Use animations or illustrations whenever possible to compliment the script.

- Use the highest quality .jpg, .gif, .bmp, png, or .tiff files you can gather.

- All images should be minimum 72 dpi, 24 -bit. Larger images allow the video editor to use the pan and zoom effects.

- Historic black and white images contrast well in the bright sunlight.

- Avoid dark images as they are difficult to see on hand-held devices.

Reprinted with permission from Catherine McCarthy Associates, 210.314.8162 (office) 210.379.6951 (mobile), catherinemcc2000@ yahoo.com

About the Author

Heidi holds a bachelor of science degree in geography from New Mexico State University and a master of science degree in recreation, parks, and tourism from West Virginia University. She has studied interpretation and tourism in Montana, West Virginia, Oregon, Chile, Costa Rica, and Greece. In 2006, she completed her master's thesis on geographic interpretation. Since that time, she has volunteered at Florissant Fossil Beds National Monument and pursued a career as a nonfiction writer. Her articles have appeared in the *Journal of Interpretation Research*, *The Interpreter*, *Legacy*, *Base Camp Colorado*, and *GSA Today*. Heidi lives in Colorado with her husband Rocco and their son Kyle.